AF556202

TEXTBOOK OF HYDROBIOLOGY

TEXTBOOK OF HYDROBIOLOGY

Dr. Rajiv Tyagi
Dept. of Zoology
M.M. College
Modi Nagar (U.P.)
(India)

DISCOVERY PUBLISHING HOUSE PVT. LTD.
NEW DELHI-110 002

First Published – 2010

Reprinted – 2017

ISBN: 978-81-8356-557-8

© Author

Textbook of Hydrobiology

Published by:

DISCOVERY PUBLISHING HOUSE PVT. LTD.

4383/4B, Ansari Road Darya Ganj
New Delhi - 110 002 (India)

Phone: +91-11-23279245, 43596064-65
Fax: +91-11-23253475

E-mail: discoverypublishinghouse@gmail.com
sales@discoverypublishinggroup.com
web: www.discoverypublishinggroup.com

Printed at:
Infinity Imaging Systems
Delhi

PREFACE

Hydrobiology is the science of life and life processes in water. Much of modern hydrobiology can be viewed as a sub-discipline of ecology but the sphere of hydrobiology includes taxonomy, economic biology, industrial biology, morphology, physiology etc. The one distinguishing aspect is that all relate to aquatic organisms. Much work is closely related to limnology and can be divided into lotic system ecology (flowing waters) and lentic system ecology (still waters).

One of the significant areas of current research is eutrophication. Special attention is paid to biotic interactions in plankton assemblage including the microbial loop, the mechanism of influencing water blooms, phosphorus load and lake turnover. Another subject of research is the acidification of mountain lakes. Long-term studies are carried out on changes in the ionic composition of the water of rivers, lakes and reservoirs in connection with acid rain and fertilization. One goal of current research is elucidation of the basic environmental functions of the ecosystem in reservoirs, which are important for water quality management and water supply.

Much of the early work of hydrobiologists concentrated on the biological processes utilised in sewage treatment and water purification especially slow sand filters. Other historically important work sought to provide biotic indices for classifying waters according to the biotic communities that they supported. This work continues to this day in Europe in the development of classification tools for assessing water bodies for the EU water framework directive.

An aquatic ecosystem is an ecosystem located in water bodies. Communities of organisms that are dependent on each other and on their environment live in aquatic ecosystems. The two main types of aquatic ecosystems are marine ecosystems and freshwater ecosystems.

—Author

CONTENTS

1

INTRODUCTION

Hydrobiology is the science of life and life processes in water. Much of modern hydrobiology can be viewed as a sub-discipline of ecology but the sphere of hydrobiology includes taxonomy, economic biology, industrial biology, morphology, physiology etc. The one distinguishing aspect is that all relate to aquatic organisms. Much work is closely related to limnology and can be divided into lotic system ecology (flowing waters) and lentic system ecology (still waters).

One of the significant areas of current research is eutrophication. Special attention is paid to biotic interactions in plankton assemblage including the microbial loop, the mechanism of influencing water blooms, phosphorus load and lake turnover. Another subject of research is the acidification of mountain lakes. Long-term studies are carried out on changes in the ionic composition of the water of rivers, lakes and reservoirs in connection with acid rain and fertilisation. One goal of current research is elucidation of the basic environmental functions of the ecosystem in reservoirs, which are important for water quality management and water supply.

Much of the early work of hydrobiologists concentrated on the biological processes utilised in sewage treatment and water purification especially slow sand filters. Other historically important work sought to provide biotic indices for classifying waters according to the biotic communities that they supported. This work continues to this day in Europe in the development of classification tools for assessing water bodies for the EU water framework directive.

An aquatic ecosystem is an ecosystem located in water bodies. Communities of organisms that are dependent on each other and on their environment live in aquatic ecosystems. The two main types of aquatic ecosystems are marine ecosystems and freshwater ecosystems.

Marine ecosystems cover approximately 71% of the Earth's surface and contain approximately 97% of the planet's water. They generate 32% of the world's net primary production. They are distinguished from freshwater ecosystems by the presence of dissolved compounds, especially salts, in the water. Approximately 85% of the dissolved materials in seawater are sodium and chlorine. Seawater has an average salinity of 35 parts per thousand (ppt) of water. Actual salinity varies among different marine ecosystems. Marine ecosystems can be divided into the following zones: oceanic (the relatively shallow part of the ocean that lies over the continental shelf); profundal (bottom or deep water); benthic (bottom substrates); intertidal (the area between high and low tides); estuaries; salt marshes; coral reefs; and hydrothermal vents (where chemosynthetic sulfur bacteria form the food base).

Classes of organisms found in marine ecosystems include brown algae, dinoflagellates, corals, cephalopods, echinoderms, and sharks. Fish caught in marine ecosystems are the biggest source of commercial foods obtained from wild populations. Environmental problems concerning marine ecosystems include unsustainable exploitation of marine resources (for example overfishing of certain species), water pollution, and building on coastal areas.

Freshwater ecosystems cover 0.8% of the Earth's surface and contain 0.009% of its total water. They generate nearly 3% of its net primary production Freshwater ecosystems contain 41% of the world's known fish species. There are three basic types of freshwater ecosystems:

- *Lentic:* slow-moving water, including pools, ponds, and lakes.
- *Lotic:* rapidly-moving water, for example streams and rivers.
- *Wetlands:* areas where the soil is saturated or inundated for at least part of the time.

Lake ecosystems can be divided into zones: *pelagic* (open offshore waters); profundal; littoral (nearshore shallow waters); and *riparian* (the area of land bordering a body of water). Two important subclasses of lakes are ponds, which typically are small lakes that intergrade with wetlands, and water reservoirs. Many lakes, or bays within them, gradually become enriched by nutrients and fill in with organic sediments, a process called eutrophication. Eutrophication is accelerated by human activity within the water catchment area of the lake.

The major zones in river ecosystems are determined by the river bed's gradient or by the velocity of the current. Faster moving turbulent water typically contains greater concentrations of dissolved oxygen, which supports greater biodiversity than the slow moving water of pools. These distinctions forms the basis for the division of rivers into upland and lowland rivers. The food base of streams within riparian forests is mostly derived from the trees, but wider streams and those that lack a canopy derive the majority of their food base from algae. Anadromous fish are also an important source of nutrients. Environmental threats to rivers include loss of water, dams, chemical pollution and introduced species.

Wetlands are dominated by vascular plants that have adapted to saturated soil. Wetlands are the most productive natural ecosystems because of the proximity of water and soil. Due to their productivity, wetlands are often converted into dry land with dykes and drains and used for agricultural purposes. Their closeness to lakes and rivers means that they are often developed for human settlement.

These are a specific type of freshwater ecosystems that are largely based on the autotroph algae which provide the base trophic level for all life in the area. The largest predator in a pond ecosystem will normally be a fish and in-between range smaller insects and microorganisms. It may have a scale of organisms from small bacteria to big creatures like water snakes, beetles, water bugs, frogs, tadpoles, and turtles.

Functions

Aquatic ecosystems perform many important environmental functions. For example, they recycle nutrients, purify water, attenuate floods, recharge ground water and provide habitats for wildlife Aquatic ecosystems are also used for human recreation, and are very important to the tourism industry, especially in coastal regions.

The health of an aquatic ecosystem is degraded when the ecosystem's ability to absorb a stress has been exceeded. A stress on an aquatic ecosystem can be a result of physical, chemical or biological alterations of the environment. Physical alterations include changes in water temperature, water flow and light availability. Chemical alterations include changes in the loading rates of biostimulatory nutrients, oxygen consuming materials, and toxins. Biological alterations include the introduction of exotic species. Human populations can impose excessive stresses on aquatic ecosystems.

Abiotic Characteristics

An ecosystem is composed of biotic communities and abiotic environmental factors, which form a self-regulating and self-sustaining unit. Abiotic environmental factors of aquatic ecosystems include temperature, salinity, and flow. The amount of dissolved oxygen in a water body is frequently the key substance in determining the extent and kinds of organic life in the water body. Fish need dissolved oxygen to survive. Conversely, oxygen is fatal to many kinds of anaerobic bacteria. The salinity of the water body is also a determining factor in the kinds of species found in the water body. Organisms in marine ecosystems tolerate salinity, while many freshwater organisms are intolerant of salt. Freshwater used for irrigation purposes often absorb levels of salt that are harmful to freshwater organisms. Though some salt can be good for organisms.

Biotic Characteristics

The organisms (also called biota) found in aquatic ecosystems are either autotrophic or heterotrophic.

Autotrophic Organisms

Autotrophic organisms are producers that generate organic compounds from inorganic material. Algae use solar energy to generate biomass from carbon dioxide and are the most important autotrophic organisms in aquatic environments Chemosynthetic bacteria are found in benthic marine ecosystems. These organisms are able to feed on hydrogen sulfide in water that comes from volcanic vents. Great concentrations of animals that feed on this bacteria are found around volcanic vents. For example, there are giant tube worms (Riftia pachyptila) 1.5m in length and clams (*Calyptogena magnifica*) 30cm long

Heterotrophic Organisms

Heterotrophic organisms consume autotrophic organisms and use the organic compounds in their bodies as energy sources and as raw materials to create their own biomass Euryhaline organisms are salt tolerant and can survive in marine ecosystems, while stenohaline or salt intolerant species can only live in freshwater environments.

ECOREGION

An ecoregion (ecological region), sometimes called a bioregion, is an ecologically and geographically defined area smaller than a "realm" or "ecozone". Ecoregions cover relatively large areas of land or water, and contain characteristic, geographically distinct assemblages of natural communities and species. The biodiversity of flora, fauna and ecosystems that characterise an ecoregion tends to be distinct from that of other ecoregions.

Definition/Delineation

An ecoregion is a "recurring pattern of ecosystems associated with characteristic combinations of soil and landform that characterise that region", researchers elaborates on this by defining ecoregions as: "areas within which there is spatial coincidence in characteristics of geographical phenomena associated with differences in the quality, health, and integrity of ecosystems Characteristics of geographical phenomena" may include geology, physiography, vegetation, climate, hydrology, terrestrial and aquatic fauna, and soils, and may or may not include the impacts of human activity (e.g. land-use patterns, vegetation changes). There is significant, but not absolute, spatial correlation among these characteristics, making the delineation of ecoregions an imperfect science. Another complication is that environmental conditions across an ecoregion boundary may change very gradually, e.g. the prairie-forest transition in the midwestern United States, making it difficult to identify an exact dividing boundary. Such transition zones are called ecotones.

Ecoregions can be delineated using an algorithmic approach or a holistic, "weight-of-evidence" approach where the importance of various factors may vary. An example of the algorithmic approach is Robert Bailey's work for the U.S. Forest Service, which uses a hierarchical classification that first divides land areas into very large regions based on climatic factors, and subdivides these regions, based first on dominant potential vegetation, and then by geomorphology and soil characteristics. The weight-of-evidence approach is exemplified by James Omernik's work for the United States Environmental Protection Agency, subsequently adopted (with modification) for North America by the Commission for Environmental Co-operation.

The intended purpose of ecoregion delineation may affect the method used. For example, the 'WWF' ecoregions were developed to aid in biodiversity conservation planning, and place a greater emphasis than the Omernik or Bailey systems on floral and faunal differences between regions. A large area of land or water that contains a geographically distinct assemblage of natural communities that:

(a) share a large majority of their species and ecological dynamics;

(b) share similar environmental conditions, and;

(c) interact ecologically in ways that are critical for their long-term persistence.

According to WWF, the boundaries of an ecoregion approximate the original extent of the natural communities prior to any major recent disruptions or changes. WWF has identified 825 terrestrial ecoregions, and approximately 450 freshwater ecoregions across the Earth.

Importance of Ecoregion

The use of the term, 'ecoregion' is an outgrowth of a surge of interest in ecosystems and their functioning. In particular, there is awareness of issues relating to spatial scale in the study and management of landscapes. It is widely recognized that interlinked ecosystems combine to form a whole that is "greater than the sum of its parts." There are many attempts to respond to ecosystems in an integrated way to achieve "multi-functional" landscapes, and various interest groups from agricultural researchers to conservationists are using the "ecoregion" as a unit of analysis.

The "Global 200" is the list of ecoregions identified by WWF as priorities for conservation.

Ecologically-based movements like bioregionalism maintain that ecoregions, rather than arbitrarily-defined political boundaries, provide a better foundation for the formation and governance of human communities, and have proposed ecoregions and watersheds as the basis for bioregional democracy initiatives.

Terrestrial Ecoregions

Terrestrial ecoregions are land ecoregions, as distinct from freshwater and marine ecoregions. In this context, terrestrial is used to mean "of land" (soil and rock), rather than the more general sense "of Earth" (which includes land and oceans).

The WWF ecologists currently divide the land surface of the Earth into eight major ecozones containing 867 smaller terrestrial ecoregions. The WWF effort is a synthesis of many previous efforts to define and classify ecoregions. Many consider this classification to be quite decisive, and some propose these as stable borders for bioregional democracy initiatives.

The eight terrestrial ecozones follow the major floral and faunal boundaries, identified by botanists and zoologists, that separate the world's major plant and animal communities. Ecozone boundaries generally follow continental boundaries, or major barriers to plant and animal distribution, like the Himalayas and the Sahara. The boundaries of ecoregions are often not as decisive or well recognized, and are subject to greater disagreement.

Ecoregions are classified by biome type, which are the major global plant communities determined by rainfall and climate. Forests, grasslands (including savanna and shrubland), and deserts (including xeric shrublands) are distinguished by climate (tropical and subtropical vs. temperate and boreal climates) and, for forests, by whether the trees are predominantly conifers (gymnosperms), or whether they are predominantly broadleaf (Angiosperms) and mixed (broadleaf and conifer). Biome types like Mediterranean forests, woodlands, and shrub, tundra, and mangroves host very distinct ecological communities, and are recognized as distinct biome types as well.

Marine Ecoregions

Marine ecoregions are regions of the world's oceans, as defined by WWF to aid in conservation activities for marine ecosystems.

The WWF/Nature Conservancy scheme groups the individual ecoregions into 12 marine realms, which represent the broad latitudinal divisions of polar, temperate, and tropical seas, with subdivisions based on ocean basins (except for the southern hemisphere temperate oceans, which are based on continents). The marine realms are subdivided into 62 marine provinces, which include one or more of the 232 marine ecoregions.

The scheme used to designate and classify marine ecoregions is analogous to that used for terrestrial ecoregions.

Major habitat types are identified: polar, temperate shelves and seas, temperate upwelling, tropical upwelling, tropical coral, pelagic (trades and westerlies), abyssal, and hadal (ocean trench. These correspond to the terrestrial biomes. Major biogeographic realms, analogous to the seven terrestrial ecozones, represent large regions of the ocean basins: North Temperate Atlantic, Eastern Tropical Atlantic, Western Tropical Atlantic, South Temperate Atlantic, North Temperate Indo-Pacific, Central Indo-Pacific, Eastern Indo-Pacific, Western Indo-Pacific, South Temperate Indo-Pacific, Southern Ocean, Antarctic, Arctic, and Mediterranean.

The classification of marine ecoregions is not developed to the same level of detail and comprehensiveness as that of the terrestrial ecoregions; only the priority conservation areas of the Global 200 are listed.

A similar system of identifying areas of the oceans for conservation purposes is the system of large marine ecosystems (LMEs), developed by the US National Oceanic and Atmospheric Administration (NOAA).

Freshwater Ecoregions

Freshwater ecoregions are the freshwater habitats of a particular geographic area, including rivers, streams, lakes, and wetlands. Freshwater ecoregions are distinct from terrestrial ecoregions, which identify biotic communities of the land, and marine ecoregions, which are biotic communities of the oceans

World Wide Fund for Nature (WWF) identifies seven major habitat types of freshwater ecoregions: Large rivers, large river headwaters, large river deltas, small rivers, large lakes, small lakes, and xeric basins.

2

Freshwater

INTRODUCTION

Freshwater is a word that refers to bodies of water such as ponds, lakes, rivers and streams containing low concentrations of dissolved salts and other total dissolved solids. In other words, the term excludes seawater and brackish water. Freshwater can also be the output of desalinated seawater. Freshwater is an important renewable resource, necessary for the survival of most terrestrial organisms, and is required by humans for drinking and agriculture, among many uses. The UN estimates that about 18 percent of the world's population lacks access to safe drinking water.

Numerical Definition

Freshwater is defined as water with less than 0.5 parts per thousand dissolved salts Freshwater bodies include lakes and ponds, rivers, some bodies of underground water and many kinds of man-made freshwater bodies, such as canals, ditches and reservoirs. The ultimate source of freshwater is the precipitation of atmosphere in the form of rain and snow.

Water Distribution

Access to unpolluted freshwater is a critical issue for the survival of many species, including humans, who must drink freshwater in order to survive. Only three per cent of the water on Earth is freshwater in nature, and about two-thirds of this is frozen in glaciers and polar ice caps. Most of the rest is underground and only 0.3 per cent is surface water. Freshwater lakes, most notably Lake Baikal in Russia and the Great Lakes in North America, contain seven-eighths of this fresh surface water. Swamps have most of the balance with only a small amount in rivers, most notably the River Amazon. The atmosphere contains 0.04% water. In areas with no freshwater on the ground surface, freshwater derived from precipitation may, because of its lower density, overlie saline ground water in lenses or layers.

AQUATIC ORGANISMS

Freshwater creates a hypotonic environment for aquatic organisms. This is problematic for some organisms, whose cell membranes will burst if excess water is not excreted. Some protists accomplish this using contractile vacuoles, while freshwater fish excrete excess water via the kidney. Although most aquatic organisms have a limited ability to regulate their osmotic balance and therefore can only live within a narrow range of salinity, diadromous fish have the ability to migrate between freshwater and saline water bodies. During these migrations they undergo changes to adapt to the surroundings of the changed salinities; these processes are hormonally controlled. The eel (*Anguilla anguilla*) uses the hormone prolactin , while in salmon (Salmo salar) the hormone cortisol plays a key role during this process.

Natural Activity against Human Activity

Freshwater is a highly valuable natural resource that has a variety of use in both human and nature activity. Freshwater is an important natural resource that allow local ecosystem of plantations of species to survive. Flows of freshwater also bring soils and nutrients that are necessary in the growth and increase of local plantation which forms food chain that ensure the food supply of local species. However, the overuse of water in human activity such as irrigation, production of products in industries and drinking water had cause a huge damage in freshwater and nature ecosystem. Changes in the contamination of freshwater results in massive diebacks of living organism, because of either too much or too little freshwater was contained in water source. The overuse of freshwater lowered the quantities of freshwater available in the freshwater ecosystem which caused the crush of balance between human society and nature. As a result, large amount of species and plantations became endangered and even extinct from the world and the local environment due to the large scale of change. Usage of freshwater must be controlled before it causes damage in environment and human society. Pollution from human activity, including oil spills, also presents a problem for freshwater resources. The largest oil spill that has ever occurred in freshwater was caused by a Shell tank ship in Magdalena, Argentina, on 15th January, 1999, polluting the environment, drinkable water, plants and animals.

Agriculture-change of Landscape

Changing landscape for the use of agriculture creates a great effect on flow of freshwater and surrounding. Reshaping a large scale of landscape in creating lands that are suitable for agriculture changed the flow and sustainability of freshwater which result in effecting the sustainability of the local ecosystem. Changes in landscape through the remove of trees and soils changed the local environments flow of freshwater and also effect the cycle of freshwater. As a result more freshwater are consumed and stored in soil which benefits agriculture. However, since agriculture was the human activity that consumes the most freshwater freshwater would be used up completely which result in scarcity and destroy of local ecosystem. Similar to events happening in Australia where too much land and freshwater flow are restructured for the use of agriculture, which ends up causing 33% of lands area at risk of salinization and scarcity Redesigning lands for the maximum use of agriculture will certainly bring a great damage to the environment and reduces the available freshwater supply since freshwater is a limiting natural resource.

Limiting Resource

Freshwater can only be renewed through the process of water cycle, where water from seas, lakes, rivers, and dams evaporates, forms clouds, and returns to water sources as precipitation. Freshwater is a renewable but limiting natural resource. As the readiness of freshwater in freshwater ecosystems lowers, nature restores it through the water cycle in the form of precipitation. However, if more freshwater is consumed through human activities than is restored by nature, the result the quantity of freshwater available in lakes, rivers, dams and underground waters is reduced which can cause serious damage to the surrounding environment.

FRESHWATER MANAGEMENT PROGRAMME

Development of freshwater managing programme helps to maintain and restore world's freshwater and freshwater ecosystem. As the world population increases more and more freshwater are needed to satisfied world demand of freshwater which reduce the quantity of available freshwater and also caused a great damage in nature environment. In order to restore the freshwater and freshwater ecosystem six steps are taken to develop the freshwater management programme. In the first step of developing freshwater management programme the flow of freshwater and the maximum amount of freshwater needed for the environment was estimated. This ensure the nature environment, local plantation and species received enough freshwater that are needed for survival. In the second step of the process influence of human activity and the amount of freshwater human needs was estimated to ensure the supply of freshwater for both drinking and human activities. In the third step the location of the place that the programme is going to take place is identify and compared to the previous estimate. By this way incorrect estimate can be corrected to ensure the environment receive the maximum amount of freshwater that it needs. In the forth step a detail outline of the plan that matches the collected data, estimation, and government's requirement were developed. In the fifth step the programme are tested in a simple freshwater experiment and results are observed to improve and also correct any mistake that occur in the plan. In the last step the planed was retested and more research was made to improve and make sure the plane function would function correctly. After that the environment's adoptability to the programme are examined to ensure the plan contribute no further damage to the environment. Freshwater management programme would certainly contribute a great effort in restoring and maintaining the world's available freshwater and freshwater ecology.

Freshwater management programme must be created through worldwide vision. In order to create a successful water management programme, the programme manager must never create the programme through an economic view. Creating a water management programme through economic point of view brought only a short term success in restoring freshwater and freshwater ecosystem. However, by having a worldwide view and consider the flow of freshwater as bloodstream of the biosphere's capacity and breath of the Earth, an efficient and effective water management programme can be created. Have a worldwide view and consider flows of freshwater as breath of the atmosphere and bloodstream of earth allows the programme manager to find out what the environment really need in restoring its freshwater and ecosystem. The worldwide view also allowed the programme manager to understand the difference between each freshwater ecosystem and helps to develop plans that will work efficiently in the environment. Worldwide view is the key to develop a successful water management programme.

Creating an effective water management programme benefit both presents and future's human society and nature environment. As the global population increase the limiting water resource will become even more limiting. The greenhouse gases produced by human will also contribute a great effect to global warming which will cause the ice and glacier in North Pole and South Pole to melt. The melt of ice will result in increase of global sea level which might cover the land and mixed with freshwater. Developing an effective water management programme helps not just in restoring the freshwater and freshwater ecosystem but also helps in reducing greenhouse gasses through the increase of plantation. Water management programme will certainly contribute a lot in restoring and maintaining global freshwater supply and nature environment.

MARINE POLLUTION

Marine pollution occurs when harmful effects, or potentially harmful effects, can result from the entry into the ocean of chemicals, particles, industrial, agricultural and residential waste, or the spread of invasive organisms. Most sources of marine pollution are land based. The pollution often comes from nonpoint sources such as agricultural runoff and wind blown debris.

Many potentially toxic chemicals adhere to tiny particles which are then taken up by plankton and benthos animals, most of which are either deposit or filter feeders. In this way, the toxins are concentrated upward within ocean food chains. Many particles combine chemically in a manner highly depletive of oxygen, causing estuaries to become anoxic. When pesticides are incorporated into the marine ecosystem, they quickly become absorbed into marine food webs. Once in the food webs, these pesticides can cause mutations, as well as diseases, which can be harmful to humans as well as the entire food web.

Toxic metals can also be introduced into marine food webs. These can cause a change tissue matter, biochemistry, behaviour, reproduction, and suppress growth in marine life. Also, many animal feeds have a high fish meal or fish hydrolysate content. In this way, marine toxins can be transferred to land animals, and appear later in meat and dairy products. Parties to the MARPOL 73/78 convention on marine pollutionAlthough marine pollution has a long history, significant international laws to counter it were enacted in the twentieth century. Marine pollution was a concern during several United Nations Conferences on the Law of the Sea beginning in the 1950s.

Most scientists believed that the oceans were so vast that they had unlimited ability to dilute, and thus render harmless, pollution. In the late 1950s and early 1960s, there were several controversies about dumping radioactive waste off the coasts of the United States by companies licensed by the Atomic Energy Commission, into the Irish Sea from the British reprocessing facility at Windscale, and into the Mediterranean Sea by the French Commissariat à l'Energie Atomique. After the Mediterranean Sea controversy, for example, Jacques Cousteau became a worldwide figure in the campaign to stop marine pollution. Marine pollution made further international headlines after the 1967 crash of the oil tanker Torrey Canyon, and after the 1969 Santa Barbara oil spill off the coast of California. Marine pollution was a major area of discussion during the 1972 United Nations Conference on the Human Environment, held in Stockholm. That year also saw the signing of the Convention on the Prevention of Marine Pollution by Dumping of Wastes and Other Matter, sometimes called the London Convention. The London Convention did not ban marine pollution, but it established black and gray lists for substances to be banned (black) or regulated by national authorities (gray). Cyanide and high-level radioactive waste, for example, were put on the black list. The London Convention applied only to waste dumped from ships, and thus did nothing to regulate waste discharged as liquids from pipelines.

PATHWAYS OF POLLUTION

There are many different ways to categorize, and examine the inputs of pollution into our marine ecosystems. Patin (n.d.) notes that generally there are three main types of inputs of pollution into the ocean: direct discharge of waste into the oceans, runoff into the waters due to rain, and pollutants that are released from the atmosphere.

One common path of entry by contaminants to the sea are rivers. The Hudson in New York State and the Raritan in New Jersey, which empty at the northern and southern ends of Staten Island, are a source of mercury contamination of zooplankton (copepods) in the open ocean. The highest concentration in the filter-feeding copepods is not at the mouths of these rivers but 70 miles south, nearer Atlantic City, because water flows close to the coast. It takes a few days before toxins are taken up by the plankton. Pollution is often classed as point source or nonpoint source pollution.

Point source pollution occurs when there is a single, identifiable, and localized source of the pollution. An example is directly discharging sewage and industrial waste into the ocean. Pollution such as this occurs particularly in developing nations. Nonpoint source pollution occurs when the pollution comes from ill-defined and diffuse sources. These can be difficult to regulate. Agricultural runoff and wind blown debris are prime examples.

Pollution from Ships

Ships can pollute waterways and oceans in many ways. Oil spills can have devastating effects. While being toxic to marine life, polycyclic aromatic hydrocarbons (PAHs), the components in crude oil, are very difficult to clean up, and last for years in the sediment and marine environment. Discharge of cargo residues from bulk carriers can pollute ports, waterways and oceans. In many instances vessels intentionally discharge illegal wastes despite foreign and domestic regulation prohibiting such actions. Ships create noise pollution that disturbs natural wildlife, and water from ballast tanks can spread harmful algae and other invasive species.

Meinesz believes that one of the worst cases of a single invasive species causing harm to an ecosystem can be attributed to a seemingly harmless jellyfish. *Mnemiopsis leidyi*, a species of comb jellyfish that spread so it now inhabits estuaries in many parts of the world. It was first introduced in 1982, and thought to have been transported to the Black Sea in a ship's ballast water. The population of the jellyfish shot up exponentially and, by 1988, it was wreaking havoc upon the local fishing industry. "The anchovy catch fell from 204,000 tons in 1984 to 200 tons in 1993; sprat from 24,600 tons in 1984 to 12,000 tons in 1993; horse mackerel from 4,000 tons in 1984 to zero in 1993." Now that the jellyfish have exhausted the zooplankton, including fish larvae, their numbers have fallen dramatically, yet they continue to maintain a stranglehold on the ecosystem.

Invasive species can take over once occupied areas, facilitate the spread of new diseases, introduce new genetic material, alter underwater seascapes and jeopardize the ability of native species to obtain food. Invasive species are responsible for about $138 billion annually in lost revenue and management costs in the US alone.

Plastic Debris

Marine debris is mainly discarded human rubbish which floats on, or is suspended in the ocean. Eighty per cent of marine debris is plastic - a component that has been rapidly accumulating since the end of World War II. The mass of plastic in the oceans may be as high as one hundred million tonnes.

Discarded plastic bags, six pack rings and other forms of plastic waste which finish up in the ocean present dangers to wildlife and fisheriesAquatic life can be threatened through entanglement, suffocation, and ingestion.Fishing nets, usually made of plastic, can be left or lost in the ocean by fishermen. Known as ghost nets, these entangle fish, dolphins, sea turtles, sharks, dugongs, crocodiles, seabirds, crabs, and other creatures, restricting movement, causing starvation, laceration and infection, and, in those that need to return to the surface to breathe, suffocation.

Many animals that live on or in the sea consume flotsam by mistake, as it often looks similar to their natural prey. Plastic debris, when bulky or tangled, is difficult to pass, and may become permanently lodged in the digestive tracts of these animals, blocking the passage of food and causing death through starvation or infection. Plastics accumulate because they don't biodegrade in the way many other substances do. They will photodegrade on exposure to the sun, but they do so properly only under dry conditions, and water inhibits this process. In marine environments, photodegraded plastic disintegrates into ever smaller pieces while remaining polymers, even down to the molecular level. When floating plastic particles photodegrade down to zooplankton sizes, jellyfish attempt to consume them, and in this way the plastic enters the ocean food chain. Many of these long-lasting pieces end up in the stomachs of marine birds and animalsncluding sea turtles, and black-footed albatross.

Plastic debris tends to accumulate at the centre of ocean gyres. In particular, the Great Pacific Garbage Patch has a very high level of plastic particulate suspended in the upper water column. In samples taken in 1999, the mass of plastic exceeded that of zooplankton (the dominant animal life in the area) by a factor of six. Toxic additives used in the manufacture of plastic materials can leech out into their surroundings when exposed to water. Waterborne hydrophobic pollutants collect and magnify on the surface of plastic debris, thus making plastic far more deadly in the ocean than it would be on land Hydrophobic contaminants are also known to bioaccumulate in fatty tissues, biomagnifying up the food chain and putting pressure on apex predators. Some plastic additives are known to disrupt the endocrine system when consumed, others can suppress the immune system or decrease reproductive rates Floating debris can also absorb persistent organic pollutants from seawater, including PCBs, DDT and PAHs Aside from toxic effects when ingested some of these are mistaken by the animal brain for estradiol, causing hormone disruption in the affected wildlife.

Toxins

Apart from plastics, there are particular problems with other toxins that do not disintegrate rapidly in the marine environment. Examples of persistent toxins are PCBs, DDT, pesticides, furans, dioxins and phenols. Heavy metals are metallic chemical elements that have a relatively high density and are toxic or poisonous at low concentrations. Examples are mercury, lead, nickel, arsenic and cadmium. Such toxins can accumulate in the tissues of many species of aquatic life in a process called bioaccumulation. They are also known to accumulate in benthic environments, such as estuaries and bay muds: a geological record of human activities of the last century.

POLLUTED LAGOON

Eutrophication is an increase in chemical nutrients, typically compounds containing nitrogen or phosphorus, in an ecosystem. It can result in an increase in the ecosystem's primary productivity (excessive plant growth and decay), and further effects including lack of oxygen and severe reductions in water quality, fish, and other animal populations. The biggest culprit are rivers that empty into the ocean, and with it the many chemicals used as fertilizers in agriculture as well as waste from livestock and humans. An excess of oxygen depleting chemicals in the water can lead to hypoxia and the creation of a dead zone.

Estuaries tend to be naturally eutrophic because land-derived nutrients are concentrated where runoff enters the marine environment in a confined channel. The World Resources Institute has identified 375 hypoxic coastal zones around the world, concentrated in coastal areas in Western Europe, the Eastern and Southern coasts of the US, and East Asia, particularly in Japan. In the ocean, there are frequent red tide algae blooms that kill fish and marine mammals and cause respiratory problems in humans and some domestic animals when the blooms reach close to shore.

In addition to land runoff, atmospheric anthropogenic fixed nitrogen can enter the open ocean. A study in 2008 found that this could account for around one third of the ocean's external (non-recycled) nitrogen supply and up to three per cent of the annual new marine biological production. It has been been suggested that accumulating reactive nitrogen in the environment may have consequences as serious as putting carbon dioxide in the atmosphere.

Acidification

The oceans are normally a natural carbon sink, absorbing carbon dioxide from the atmosphere. Because the levels of atmospheric carbon dioxide are increasing, the oceans are becoming more acidic The potential consequences of ocean acidification are not fully understood, but there are concerns that structures made of calcium carbonate may become vulnerable to dissolution, affecting corals and the ability of shellfish to form shells.

A report from NOAA scientists (2008) found that large amounts of relatively acidified water are upwelling to within four miles of the Pacific continental shelf area of North America. This area is a critical zone where most local marine life lives or is born. While the paper dealt only with areas from Vancouver to northern California, other continental shelf areas may be experiencing similar effects. Specific examples are as follows:

- Chinese and Russian industrial pollution such as phenols and heavy metals in the Amur River have devastated fish stocks and damaged its estuary soil.
- Wabamun Lake in Alberta, Canada, once the best whitefish lake in the area, now has unacceptable levels of heavy metals in its sediment and fish.
- Acute and chronic pollution events have been shown to impact southern California kelp forests, though the intensity of the impact seems to depend on both the nature of the contaminants and duration of exposure.
- Ballast water taken up at sea and released in port is a major source of unwanted exotic marine life. The invasive freshwater zebra mussels, native to the Black, Caspian and Azov seas, were probably transported to the Great Lakes via ballast water from a transoceanic vessel.
- Due to their high position in the food chain and the subsequent accumulation of heavy metals from their diet, mercury levels can be high in larger species such as bluefin and albacore. As a result, in March 2004 the United States FDA issued guidelines recommending that pregnant women, nursing mothers and children limit their intake of tuna and other types of predatory fish.
- Some shellfish and crabs can survive polluted environments, accumulating heavy metals or toxins in their tissues. For example, mitten crabs have a

remarkable ability to survive in highly modified aquatic habitats, including polluted waters The farming and harvesting of such species needs careful management if they are to be used as a food.

- Mining has a poor environmental track record. For example, according to the United States Environmental Protection Agency, mining has contaminated portions of the headwaters of over 40% of watersheds in the western continental US. Much of this pollution finishes up in the sea.
- Heavy metals enter the environment through oil spills- such as the Prestige oil spill on the Galician coast - or from other natural or anthropogenic sources.

Solutions

Marine pollution is part of the problem of too much pollution by humans in general. There are only two ways to remedy this: either the human population is reduced, or the ecological footprint left behind by the average human is reduced. If we do not follow the second way, then the first way may be imposed upon us, as world ecosystems falter and cease to support us.

The second way is for us, individually, to consume and pollute less than we do currently. For this there must be social and political will, together with a shift in awareness, so more people respect their environment and are less disposed to abuse it. At an operational level, regulations, and international government participation is needed. It is often very difficult to regulate marine pollution because pollution spreads over international barriers, thus making regulations hard to create as well as enforce.

Perhaps the most important strategy for reducing marine pollution is education. Most are unaware of the sources, and harmful effects of marine pollution, and therefore little is done to address the situation. In order to inform the population of all the facts, in depth research must be done to provide the full scale of the situation. Then this information must be made public.

One of the reasons why environmental concern is lacking among the Chinese is because the public awareness is low and therefore should be targeted. Likewise, regulation, based upon such in-depth research should be employed. In California, such regulations have already been put in place to protect Californian coastal waters from agricultural runoff. This includes the California Water Code, as well as several voluntary programmes. Similarly, in India, several tactics have been employed that help reduce marine pollution, however, they do not significantly target the problem. In Chennai city, India, sewage has been dumped further into open waters. Due to the mass of waste being deposited, open-ocean is best for diluting, and dispersing pollutants, thus making them less harmful to marine ecosystems.

ECOLOGY OF FRESH-WATER

Streams, lakes, and wetlands differ profoundly from one another in the conditions they provide as habitats for biological communities. Fundamental characteristics of standing water (a lentic system) or flowing water (a lotic system), the dynamics of its interaction with adjacent land and vegetation, and seasonal fluctuations in water conditions determine characteristic biological assemblages.

Streams

The most apparent feature of streams is flowing water. The geomorphology and topography through which streams flow, their channel steepness, the variability in stream-bottom substrates, and the availability of woody debris are among the natural controls that influence flow patterns. The diversity in physical structure and flow among riffles, pools, and glides is reflected in equally diverse aquatic communities. In flat valley floodplains, streams naturally meander, or flow in a winding path. In these systems, flooding is an important natural process: nutrient-rich sediments are deposited onto the floodplain, and young fish are protected in quieter areas away from high flow. Terrestrial (land-based) invertebrates become important sources of food during these times. Under the stream and beneath floodplain soils, water flows in the subsurface in the hyporheic zone. Waters are cooled, nutrients are exchanged, and invertebrates are specially adapted to live in this subterranean habitat.

A river basin consists of its entire upstream network: its watershed is the landscape, including the stream network and the land it traverses. Riparian (streamside) zones make up the transition between stream and terrestrial environment, encompassing the area where vegetation and streams interact. Riparian plants provide shade, cool the stream, retain soils, and filter nutrients. Fallen leaves decompose and provide nutrients for stream microorganisms and invertebrates. Changing habitats along the longitudinal stream gradient, from its headwaters to downstream reaches, can be thought of as a stream continuum. Energy possessed by the stream and aquatic communities tend to follow this continuum in predictable ways. Leafy inputs are most important in headwaters, whereas algae are more important as a food base in wider, more sunlit reaches. Nutrients released from streambanks and within the stream are taken up by algae in a downstream spiral of repeated uptake and release.

Macro-invertebrates in the stream continuum are classified into functional feeding groups, depending on how they obtain food. In headwaters, shredding invertebrates, dependent on decomposing leaves, are common. As streams open up, scraping macroinvertebrates that scoop algae off rocks are more abundant. Collector invertebrates either gather or filter out small edible particles everywhere, but in wide, deep rivers they dominate with plankton. As adults many stream invertebrates move into the terrestrial environment.

In stream food webs, primary production (the foundation of food chains) comes from riparian inputs and algae, and most invertebrates are herbivores or detritivores. Top predators are primarily fish but also include birds, amphibians, and humans. Invertebrate predators are relatively few. Fish move easily between habitats, and many feed on both stream and riparian invertebrates. A few birds spear large invertebrates that avoid fish predation. Other birds and bats capture adult aquatic insects that emerge from the stream.

Lakes

Lakes are characterized by basin shape, volume, and depth. Shallow edges where rooted vegetation persists are nursery grounds for fish and diverse invertebrates. The open-water (pelagic) zone is classified into layers, depending on the degree of mixing that occurs. Water changes density with temperature, causing lakes to become layered, or stratified, into temperature zones. Consequently, significant energy is needed to mix a lake's thermal layers. Deep lakes are stratified into a warmer, upper layer that mixes readily (epilimnion); a middle layer of quickly changing temperatures (metalimnion); and a deep, cool bottom layer that mixes infrequently during the year (hypolimnion). Wind easily mixes shallow lakes, so these layers either do not persist or do not develop.

Phytoplankton, predominantly algae, form the base of a lake's food chain. These primary producers fall into five major categories (see table). These major categories also are represented in streams. A community of microscopic zooplankton lives in a lake's upper layer, feeding on single-celled or small colonial algae. In clear, relatively unproductive lakes, zooplankton consume much of the algae. Very productive lakes are much less clear, with abundant algae in blooms of filamentous forms.

Diatoms (Bacillariophyta): Primary pigments are chlorophyll and carotenes so they appear yellow-brown in color, have cell walls made from silica, often have early season dominance, cell walls may persist for thousands of years in sediments where they are useful for determining historic water characteristics.

Green Algae (Chlorophyta): Primary pigment is chlorophyll so they appear bright green, population growth often follows spring diatoms, are important food for zooplankton, occasionally cause nuisance blooms especially when nitrogen concentrations in the lake are high.

Golden Algae (Chrysophyta): Primary pigments are chlorophyll, carotene and xanthophylls, appear yellow-brown in colour, optimize their growth during the relatively cool waters of late winter/early spring, taste and odor problems are often associated with golden algae, may supplement photosynthesis by capturing food particles in the water.

Blue-Green Algae (Cyanobacteria): Primary pigments are chlorophyll, carotene, phycobilins, and xanthophylls, appear blue-green, no chloroplasts-color is distributed evenly throughout cell, are similar biologically to bacteria, often form filamentous or spherical colonies, can form nuisance blooms, often dominate summer plankton of productive lakes, most can regulate their buoyancy, many are nitrogen-fixers, some produce potent toxins.

Dinoflagellates (Dinophyta): Appear dark green to brown to almost black in color, are free-swimming, have two flagella, have forward-spiraling swimming motion, blooms are associated with organic pollution, may cause taste and odor problems in water, marine dinoflagellates are responsible for "red tides".

Water chemistry plays an important role in lake dynamics, as nutrients influence algal productivity and higher trophic levels. In deep lakes, the bottom layer has little oxygen when it is not mixing, and few organisms survive there. Similarly, very salty lakes contain only a few highly specialized zooplankton.

Fish are visual predators and select prey on the basis of size. They consume the largest zooplankton, and remaining zooplankton will be small. A trophic cascade occurs as the top predators (fish) depress the next trophic level (zooplankton), releasing high production in a third level (algae). In fishless lakes, invertebrate predators dominate, and large herbivorous zooplankton escape predation.

Wetlands

Wetlands generally are more shallow than lakes and have standing or flowing water above, near, or below the surface. They vary in size, from puddles to thousands of hectares (a hectare is 10,000 square meters). Because water is not necessarily present year-round, characteristic waterlogged soils or plants help identify their location and extent. Wetlands often are intermediate habitats, representing a transition between aquatic and terrestrial habitats. Their transitional position makes them key exporters of organic materials and sinks for nutrients. Persistent, shallow standing water forms a permanent wetland. When soils are saturated for only part of the year, temporary or ephemeral wetlands are created.

Wetland communities reflect the duration and depth of standing water. Plants vary specifically in requirements for annual wetness. Similarly, invertebrates differ in intervals required to mature, eventually migrating or becoming dormant in the dry season. Some amphibians use only a seasonal aquatic habitat before migrating; others require continuous wetlands. Ephemeral plant and invertebrate resources will attract migratory waterfowl, but resident birds and fish require year-round water. Thus, a variety of wetlands support diverse plant and animal communities.

Human Influences

Habitat loss due to human activities has severely affected fresh-water ecosystems. Because of filling and draining activities more than half (53%) of wetlands in the continental United States were lost between 1780 and 1980. Dams, channellization, wood removal, and flow alteration have reduced stream habitat significantly. Profound changes from accidental and intentional introduction of nonnative plant and animal species have altered aquatic communities and destroyed habitats. Acid rain and other consequences of air and water pollution have severely damaged lakes, streams, and wetlands. Cumulative effects of these activities often result in declining native flora and fauna. Although scientists and decisionmakers recognize many alterations caused by humans, they have just begun to develop scientific and political understandings for fresh-water restoration.

3

LIFE IN WATER

INTRODUCTION

Life is thought to have originated in an aquatic environment—the oceans. Living organisms have since adapted to numerous aquatic habitats, both marine and fresh-water. They occupy environments as diverse as lakes, rivers, and oceans.

MARINE ENVIRONMENT

About 17 per cent of known biological species live in oceans. Marine species are described as either pelagic or benthic. Pelagic organisms live in the water column itself. Benthic species live on the ocean bottom.

Pelagic

Pelagic organisms include plankton, which float along with currents, and nekton, which are active swimmers. Plankton are divided into phytoplankton, which include photosynthesizing species such as algae, and zooplankton, which are consumer species. Zooplankton consist largely of copepods (tiny crustaceans). Although plankton generally drift with ocean currents, some plankton have limited mobility. For example, certain zooplankton species move towards the water surface at night to feed, when there is less danger of predation, and return to deeper waters during the day. Organisms that are planktonic throughout their life cycles are known as holoplankton. Organisms that are only planktonic during the early parts of their life cycles are called meroplankton. Meroplankton include the larval or juvenile forms of many species of fish and mollusks. These species use the planktonic stage to disperse to new areas. Although most planktonic species are small, some are large, such as kelp and jellyfish.

Nekton are active swimmers that use diverse means to propel themselves through the water. Some species swim using fins, tails, or flippers. Other species, such as mussels, move by shooting out jets of water, known as jet propulsion. Nektonic species include fish, octopus, sea turtles, whales, seals, penguins, and many others. Many nektonic species eat high in the food chain, although there are plankton-eating species (e.g., some fish) and herbivorous species (e.g., sea turtles) in addition to carnivorous ones (e.g., seals and killer whales). Pelagic marine species may also be categorized according to the depths at which they occur. Different water depths are characterized by differences in temperature, amount of sunlight received, and availability of nutrients. The epipelagic zone describes oceanic waters closest to the surface, and is the zone richest in marine life. In the epipelagic zone, there is enough sunlight for photosynthesis. For that reason, the epipelagic zone is also called the photic (light) zone. All photosynthetic species, including the phytoplankton, live in this zone, as do many of the species that feed on phytoplankton.

Below the photic zone is the aphotic zone, which is characterized by very limited light (or no light) and limited food. Species in the aphotic zone often depend on food drifting down from above. Consequently, there are many detritivores (species that feed on dead or decaying organic matter) in these habitats.

Certain deep-sea habitats can be highly diverse. In the deep-sea vents, for example, chemosynthetic bacteria (rather than photosynthetic species) form the basis of the food chain. These bacteria obtain nergy from chemical sources such as hydrogen sulfide instead of from sunlight.

Benthic

Benthic species live on the ocean bottoms, and represent the greatest proportion of marine species; in fact, 98 percent of marine species are benthic. Benthic species include epifauna, which live on the surface, and infauna, which burrow into seafloor sediment. Benthic epifauna include species such as oysters, scallops, sea stars, crabs, and lobsters. Examples of infauna include clams and many species of worms. Some benthic species are sessile (non-moving), and live attached to the ocean bottom. Benthic plants generally are found only in shallow waters where there is enough sunlight for photosynthesis. However, benthic animals are found at a wide variety of depths, including in the deepest parts of the ocean. Some species, such as flounder, are capable of both benthic and nektonic existence.

Distance from Shore

The distance of a zone from shore can categorize marine environments. The neritic zone describes coastal marine regions. The neritic zone is particularly rich with life because the relatively shallow water allows for plentiful photosynthesis, and because a steady flow of nutrients is washed into the water from land. Farther from land, areas of open ocean are described as the oceanic zone. The oceanic zone has significantly less total biomass than the neritic zone. The intertidal zone is the area of shore that alternates between being submerged and dry, depending on the level of the tide. Numerous species are specialized for living in the intertidal zone, including the familiar barnacles. The intertidal zone has the greatest density of living organisms among marine environments.

Fresh-water Environment

Fresh-water habitats are extremely diverse, and include both still-water environments like lakes and ponds, and flowing-water environments like rivers and streams.

Still-water Habitats

Such as oceans, lakes have pelagic and benthic zones. The temperature of lake water varies depending on depth, and can also change dramatically over seasons. The epilimnion is the topmost layer of lake water. It is significantly warmer than deeper areas due to heating by sunlight. The hypolimnion layer describes deeper, colder lake water. Many of the nutrients in lakes collect at lake bottoms.

Turnover occurs when all the water in a lake is nearly thermally uniform and mixed, distributing nutrients throughout the water. Turnover occurs twice a year in many temperate lakes, but may occur only once in subtropical environments, or not at all in permanently stratified lakes.

Lakes also can be described as either oligotrophic or eutrophic (or in between these two extremes). Oligotrophic lakes have low levels of nutrients and low productivity. They generally contain cold, highly oxygenated water and support species adapted to these conditions. Eutrophic lakes, on the other hand, have plentiful nutrients and are highly productive. Species that inhabit eutrophic lakes must be tolerant of low oxygen levels and warm temperatures. In general, oxygen levels in lakes depend on the amount of water circulation, the surface area that is exposed to air, and levels of oxygen consumption by living organisms.

FLOWING-WATER HABITATS

River species generally have special adaptations for living in water currents. Some species are sessile and live anchored to the river bottom. Other species have evolved adaptations such as suckers or hooks to keep themselves from being washed away. Still other species are strong swimmers. Many of these have flattened bodies that help them resist the pressure of the current.

Compared to lakes, rivers tend to be well-oxygenated because of the constant motion of the water. Temperatures can change quickly in rivers, but do not span as great a range as in lakes or other still water. Because there is less penetration of light in flowing water, plant diversity is generally lower in rivers than in lakes. As in other aquatic ecosystems, algae frequently occupy the base of the food chain.

CHALLENGES OF AQUATIC LIFE

Flotation

Flotation or placement in the water column is a challenge faced by all aquatic organisms. For example, it is crucial to phytoplankton to stay in the photic zone, where there is access to sunlight. The small size of most phytoplankton, plus a special oily substance in the cytoplasm of cells, helps keep these organisms afloat.

Zooplankton use a variety of techniques to stay close to the water surface. These include the secretion of oily or waxy substances, possession of air-filled sacs similar to the swim bladders of fish, and special appendages that assist in floating. Some zooplankton even tread water.

Fish have special swim bladders, which they fill with gas to lower their body density. By keeping their body at the same density as water, a state called neutral buoyancy, fish are able to move freely up and down.

Salinity

Aquatic species also have to deal with salinity, the level of salt in the water. Some marine species, including sharks and most marine invertebrates, simply maintain the same salinity level in their tissues as is in the surrounding water. Some marine vertebrates, however, have lower salinity in their tissues than is in sea water. These species have a tendency to lose water to the environment. They make up for this by drinking sea water and excreting excess salt through their gills.

Fresh-water aquatic species have the opposite problem—a tendency to absorb too much water. These species must constantly expel water, which they do by excreting a dilute urine. Species that occupy both fresh water and marine habitats at different stages of their life cycle must transition between two modes of maintaining water balance. Salmon hatch in fresh water, mature in the ocean, and return to fresh-water habitats to spawn. Eels, on the other hand, hatch in salt water, migrate to fresh-water environments where they mature, and return to the ocean to spawn.

Salinity is particularly variable in coastal waters, because oceans receive variable amounts of fresh water from rivers and other sources. Species in coastal habitats must be tolerant of salinity changes and are described as euryhaline. In the open ocean, salinity levels are generally constant, and species that live there cannot tolerate salinity changes. These organisms are described as stenohaline.

Temperature

Eurythermal species are those that can survive in a variety of temperatures. Eurythermality generally characterizes species that live near the water surface, where temperatures change depending on the seasons or the time of day. Species that occupy deeper waters generally experience more constant temperatures, are intolerant of temperature changes, and are described as stenothermal.

ALGAL BLOOMS IN FRESH WATER

Aquatic ecologists are concerned with blooms (very high cell densities) of algae in reservoirs, lakes, and streams because their occurrence can have ecological, aesthetic, and human health impacts. In waterbodies used for water supply, algal blooms can cause physical problems (e.g., clogging screens) or can cause taste and odor problems in waters used for drinking. Blooms involving toxin-producing species can pose serious threats to animals and humans.

Algae in Aquatic Ecosystems

The term "algae" is generally used to refer to a wide variety of different and dissimilar photosynthetic organisms, generally microscopic. Depending on the species, algae can inhabit fresh or salt water. In modern taxonomic systems, algae are usually assigned to one of six divisions. The misnamed blue-green algae are often grouped with algae because of the chloroplasts contained within the cells. However, these organisms are actually photosynthetic bacteria assigned to the group cyanobacteria. Fresh-water algae, also called phytoplankton, vary in shape and color, and are found in a large range of habitats, such as ponds, lakes, reservoirs, and streams. They are a natural and essential part of the ecosystem. In these habitats, the phytoplankton are the base of the aquatic food chain. Small fresh-water crustaceans and other small animals consume the phytoplankton and in turn are consumed by larger animals.

BLOOM OCCURRENCES AND IMPACT

Under certain conditions, several species of true algae as well as the cyanobacteria are capable of causing various nuisance effects in fresh water, such as excessive accumulations of foams, scums, and discoloration of the water. When the numbers of algae in a lake or a river increase explosively, an algal "bloom" is the result. Lakes, ponds, and slow-moving rivers are most susceptible to blooms.

Algal blooms are natural occurrences, and may occur with regularity (e.g., every summer), depending on weather and water conditions. The likelihood of a bloom depends on local conditions and characteristics of the particular body of water. Blooms generally occur where there are high levels of nutrients present, together with the occurrence of warm, sunny, calm conditions. However, human activity often can trigger or accelerate algal blooms. Natural sources of nutrients such as phosphorus or nitrogen compounds can be supplemented by a variety of human activities. For example, in rural areas, agricultural runoff from fields can wash fertilizers into the water. In urban areas, nutrient sources can include treated wastewaters from septic systems and sewage treatment plants, and urban stormwater runoff that carries nonpoint-source pollutants such as lawn fertilizers.

An algal bloom contributes to the natural "aging" process of a lake, and in some lakes can provide important benefits by boosting primary productivity. But in other cases, recurrent or severe blooms can cause dissolved oxygen depletion as the large numbers of dead algae decay. In highly eutrophic (enriched) lakes, algal blooms may lead to anoxia and fish kills during the summer. In terms of human values, the odors and unattractive appearance of algal blooms can detract from the recreational value of reservoirs, lakes, and streams. Repeated blooms may cause property values of lakeside or riverside tracts to decline.

Toxic Blooms

Some algae produce toxic chemicals that pose a threat to fish, other aquatic organisms, wild and domestic animals, and humans. The toxins are released into the water when the algae die and decay. The most common and visible nuisance algae in fresh water, and the species that are often toxic, are the cyanobacteria. A cyanobacterial bloom will form on the surface and can accumulate downwind, forming a thick scum that sometimes resembles paint floating on the water. Because these mats are blown close to shore, humans and wild and domestic animals can come into contact with the unsightly material.

Blooms of toxic species of algae and cyanobacteria can flood the water environment with the biotoxin they produce. When toxic, blooms can cause human illnesses such as gastroenteritis (if the toxin is ingested) and lung irritations (if the toxin becomes aerosolized and hence airborne). Other cyanobacterial toxins are less drastic, and cause skin irritation to people who swim through an algal bloom. Toxicity can sometimes cause severe illness and death to animals that consume the biotoxin-containing water. Cyanobacterial toxins are known to affect bean photosynthesis when they are present in irrigation water. The toxins also can modify zooplankton communities, reduce growth of trout, and interfere with development of fish and amphibians. In some cases, toxins can be bioconcentrated by fresh-water clams.

Microcystins comprise the most common group of about fifty cyanobacterial toxins. Among these toxins are ones that, if ingested in sufficient quantity, can harm the liver (hepatotoxins) or nervous system (neurotoxins). Microcystins can persist in water because they are stable in both hot and cold water. Even boiling the water, which makes the water safe from harmful bacteria, will not destroy microcystins. As a result of this threat, the Canadian government implemented a recommended water-quality guideline of 1.5 µg per liter of microsystin-LR (the most common hepatotoxin), and other countries will likely follow suit.

In Canada as well as the United States, there are few reports of injury and no reports of human deaths resulting from microcystins in drinking water, in large part because surface-water sources of drinking water (e.g., reservoirs, lakes, and rivers) must undergo filtration and chlorination at water utilities prior to being distributed to customers. (Cyanobacterial toxins can be removed from water only by activated charcoal filters and chlorination.)

Control Considerations

Repeated episodes of algal blooms can be an indication that a river or lake is being contaminated, or that other aspects of a lake's ecology are out of balance. While cyanobacterial blooms receive the most public and scientific attention, the excessive growth of other algae and other aquatic plants also can cause significant degradation of a lake or pond, particularly in waters receiving sewage or agricultural runoff. Aquatic biologists and other water-quality specialists often are called to identify the causes and recommend management steps to reduce or control the problem. However, prevention of a problem is always better than trying to fix the problem after it happens.

Controlling agricultural, urban, and stormwater runoff; properly maintaining septic systems; and properly managing residential applications of fertilizers are probably the most effective measures that can be taken to help prevent human-induced fresh-water algal blooms.

ALGAL BLOOMS IN THE OCEAN

The ocean, that vast body of water covering 71 per cent of the Earth's surface, is divided into four major basins: the Pacific, Atlantic, Indian, and Arctic Oceans. These large basins are interconnected with various shallow seas, such as the Mediterranean Sea, the Gulf of Mexico, and the South China Sea. Oceans and seas abound with life, ranging from microscopic unicellular (one-celled) organisms to multicellular (many-celled) animals. Algae is an important life form in the ocean. Life in the ocean is maintained in balance by forces of nature and by predator–prey relationships, unless some external pressures upset the balance. When a balance upset leads to conditions more favorable for the reproduction and growth of algae, an explosive increase in the number of algal cell density occurs Such rapid increases in the algae population are called algal blooms.

During a bloom, a litre of water may contain millions of algae. The most widely publicized type of algal bloom is associated with species that produce a toxin (chemical substance) harmful to animals that feed on the algae (and hence is known as a harmful algal bloom), and/or algae that cause a tint in the water because of the photosynthetic pigments they contain. The latter commonly is known as a "red tide", but different pigments can turn the water red, brown, purple, orange, or yellow. Depending on the circumstances and the species present, a red tide may or may not be harmful. Although not all algal blooms in the ocean produce highly visible effects nor are all blooms harmful, they nonetheless affect life in the ocean and on land in both beneficial and harmful ways.

Requirements for a Bloom

Algae require warmth, sunlight, and nutrients to grow and reproduce, so they live in the upper 60 to 90 metres (200 to 300 feet) of ocean water. The upper layer of water, the epipelagic zone, is rich in oxygen, penetrated by sunlight, and warmer than water at lower levels. As algae and other organisms that live in the ocean die, they fall to the bottom of the ocean, where they decay and release the compounds from which they were made. Under certain conditions, these nutrients can deplete the oxygen in the water. Temperature and salt concentration determine the density of water and how water moves (currents). Cold water is denser (heavier) and sinks from the surface (downwelling). Other water moves across to replace it. Eventually, water at the surface is replaced by water that has risen, or upwelled, from the bottom to the surface somewhere else in the ocean. These upwellings bring nutrient-rich waters to the top. This increase in nutrients can trigger algae blooms.

An increase in nutrients also may be caused by activities of humans, such as runoff from animal farms or fertilized croplands and lawns, or atmospheric deposition of sulfur and nitrogen compounds or oxides derived from the burning of fossil fuel. These nutrients lead to blooms in coastal waters to a greater extent than in the open ocean. However, some of these nutrients do find their way to the open ocean far from shore, and contribute to the formation of blooms in the open ocean. Their movement is aided by the wind and by ocean currents. Algae blooms in the open ocean are not usually harmful; instead, they provide many benefits, largely deriving from the fact that the open ocean is relatively unproductive (low in nutrients).

Algae and Photosynthesis

Algae are referred to as plants because, like plants, they produce organic compounds from inorganic compounds (carbon dioxide and water) by capturing and using the energy from sunlight. Most algae are eukaryotic, an exception being the blue-green algae (cyanobacteria). Photosynthesis takes place in organelles called chloroplasts in eukaryotic cells. Chloroplasts contain an outer and an inner membrane and pancakeshaped structures called thylakoids. Energy is captured from sunlight by pigments (chlorophylls a and b and carotenoids) stored in the thylakoids.

Photosynthesis occurs in two stages commonly referred to as the light reactions (light is required) and the dark reactions (no light is directly required). During the light reactions, energy captured from sunlight is used to split (dissociate) water molecules. Electrons released from this reaction are passed down a series of electron carrier molecules, leading to the storage of the energy in the form of ATP (adenosine triphosphate). This is the form in which living organisms store energy to be used immediately for carrying out chemical reactions and other activities.

Oxygen is produced as a byproduct of the light reactions. During the dark reactions (Calvin cycle), six molecules of carbon dioxide are used to make sugar (glucose). Because algae use carbon dioxide and release oxygen as a product of the light reactions, these plants play an important role in maintaining the proper concentrations of carbon dioxide and oxygen in the environment, via the carbon cycle and oxygen cycle.

Algae, such as green plants, produce the first organic compounds in the food chain and thus are referred to as primary producers. Other organisms cannot use inorganic molecules to make the organic compounds that they need for life, and therefore depend on algae and other plants as the initial source of organic compounds. These organisms either eat algae to obtain organic compounds, or obtain them from the water when they are released after the algae die.

Cyanobacteria

Cyanobacteria, also known as blue-green algae, are one of the oldest known types of algae and are believed to have played a major role in the addition of oxygen to the Earth's early atmosphere. Some cyanobacteria carry out nitrogen fixation, which is the conversion of nitrogen gas into nitrogen compounds that can be used by other primary producers.

Diatoms

Diatoms are unicellular and have a cell wall composed of silica, a glass-like material, which comprises a shell-like structure called a frustule.

When diatoms die, the frustules settle to the bottom of the ocean floor and combine with the soil to form diatomaceous earth. Diatomaceous earth is used in products such as filters for swimming pools, as temperature and sound insulators, and as an abrasive in toothpaste.

Dinoflagellates

Dinoflagellates have two unequal flagella that help them direct their movement. Many of these organisms contain colored pigments that cause the water to appear colored when these organisms bloom, leading to the terms "red tide" or "brown tide," for example. Some dinoflagellates live in close association with marine animals, such as sponges, sea anemones, giant clams, and corals. The golden-brown photosynthetic cells found in these animals, called zooxanthellae, actually are dinoflagellates.

COCCOLITHOPHORES

Coccolithophores are cells covered with button-like structures called coccoliths made of calcium carbonate. The coccoliths give the ocean a milky white or turquoise appearance during intense blooms. The long-term flux of coccoliths to the ocean floor is the main process responsible for the formation of chalk and limestone. Coccolithophores and some other algae participate in the sulfur cycle and produce the gas dimethyl sulfide. This is the primary way that sulfur is carried between ocean and land.

Dimethyl sulfide leaves the surface of the water and reacts with oxygen in the atmosphere to form tiny sulfuric acid droplets. These droplets are carried over land and fall back to land in the form of precipitation. They also aid in the formation of clouds, which partially block the transmission of harmful ultraviolet light that penetrates the surface water. Cloud formation also is thought to encourage surface winds that promote the movement of surface water, leading to upwellings that bring nutrients to the surface.

Benefits of Algal Blooms

Algal blooms provide large concentrations of algae that produce organic compounds needed by higher organisms, ranging from oysters, clams, and mussels to human beings. For this reason, productivity increases in areas where algal blooms occur. More algae in the water means that more carbon dioxide is used from the atmosphere and that more oxygen is released into the atmosphere. Oxygen is necessary for many living things, including humans. As noted previously, the production of dimethyl sulfide gas helps protect algae from harmful ultraviolet rays so they remain healthy and thus are able to continue the cycle of sustaining life on Earth.

Even in the coldest parts of the ocean, algae provide the primary source of organic material to animals at the bottom of the food chain. Organic materials are moved up the food chain as higher organisms feed on those lower down the chain. For example, algae have been found in Antarctic sea ice. As sea water freezes, algae living in the water are frozen in the ice, where they later can be released during a thaw. These algae are a vital source of food for krill, the shrimp-like organisms eaten by penguins, seals, seabirds, and whales.

4

LAKES BIOLOGICAL PROCESSES

INTRODUCTION

The aquatic environment is shaped by complex interactions among a variety of physical, chemical, and biological factors. For example, physical factors such as climate, land topography, bedrock geology, and soil type influence the amount of water flowing in streams and discharging to lakes, as well as the types of materials (chemicals and particulates) found in the water. In turn, these physical and chemical factors support a community of biological organisms unique to a water environment.

Light

The presence and abundance of light in lakes control many biological processes. Green plants convert the light energy of the Sun into chemical energy (and ultimately plant tissue) through a process called photosynthesis. As sunlight strikes water, it is reflected from the surface (much like a mirror), scattered by particles in the water, and absorbed by the water itself. Gradually, much of the light gets used up until there is not enough light energy remaining at depth to support plant photosynthesis.

The surface depths of a lake that receive sufficient light to allow photosynthesis make up the euphotic zone. The lower limit of the euphotic zone is approximated by the one per cent light level, or that depth where only one per cent of the surface sunlight remains. The depth of the euphotic may be a little as 1 meter (3 feet) in very turbid (cloudy) lakes to as much as 31 metres (100 feet) in very clear lakes.

Aquatic Communities

The shallow, nearshore waters of the lake where light penetrates all the way to the bottom is called the littoral zone (see the figure). The littoral community is considered the most diverse and abundant biological community in lakes. In the littoral community, plants (macrophytes) rooted in the sediments receive enough light to grow. Some rooted plants (emergents), such as cattails, emerge from the water surface. Other plants (floating-leaved), such as water lilies, have leaves that float on the surface. Still other plants (submergents) stay entirely submerged. The diversity of plants and the structure they add to the littoral zone attract an abundance of aquatic life. Many fish build nests here, and young fish find protection among the plants from predators.

A multitude of aquatic insects (food for many fish) live on and feed among the plants and sediments of the littoral. Turtles, frogs, and many other aquatic organisms call the littoral community home. The zone of open, deeper water found farther out from the littoral zone is the pelagic community. Here, light is still abundant, and the waters are frequently mixed by wind. Tiny, free-floating plants and animals (plankton) live here along with cruising fish. The deep open water beneath the pelagic and euphotic zone is the profundal zone. The lack of light does not allow plants to grow here, but many fish and tiny crustaceans may still live here. Along the bottom of the lake lies the benthic zone. A variety of bottom-dwelling organisms—catfish, mollusks, worms, and midge larvae—live in this benthic community and derive their food from the sediments.

Living in the Water

Water is a medium of extreme properties that strongly shape the nature of the organisms that can survive in it. Thus, life in the water requires special adaptations. Oxygen, plentiful in the atmosphere for land animals, is much less abundant in water. Air-breathing aquatic organisms must have specialized and efficient mechanisms, such as gills, to extract oxygen from water. Except for benthic organisms that live on the lake or stream bottom, most aquatic organisms require some means to regulate their buoyancy so that they can remain suspended in the water. Many fish have air bladders, lightweight bones, and scales—all adaptations to increase buoyancy.

Plankton may have long spines or elaborate shapes to increase their surface area which slows down their sinking rate. Because ponds or streams may dry up, many aquatic organisms can enter a resting stage during development or may aestivate, as some amphibians may do in summer drought. On the other hand, the annual range in natural water temperatures (approximately 0 to 30°C, or 32 to 86°F in temperate areas) is much lower than the range that land plants and animals must face (-28 to 40°C, or -18 to 104°F).

FOOD WEB

Aquatic plants and animals interact with each other through a series of interconnecting pathways called a food web. Each different level in the food web or chain is called a trophic level because each represents a different type of productivity. The schematic below illustrates the food web and microbial loop for the pelagic zone of a typical fresh-water lake. Microbes are important in enabling and sustaining nutrient cycles.

Phytoplankton (predominantly algae), like terrestrial plants, require sunlight, water, and nutrients for photosynthesis. The algae and rooted macrophytes are primary producers in the aquatic environment. By converting light energy into chemical energy via photosynthesis, they create food (energy) needed for the entire aquatic food web. As such, they are at the base of the food chain. Algal groups are organized generally by color, such as green algae, yellow-brown algae, and so on. Zooplankton, such as the shrimp-like Daphnia and Bosmina, are the primary consumers because they eat the primary producers. Zooplankton are considered herbivores because they consume plant material and are the functional equivalent of cows or rabbits on land. Planktivores are organisms that eat zooplankton. Aquatic organisms that are planktivorous include fish, such as minnows, small sunfish, and gizzard shad, as well as a variety of aquatic insect larvae.

The piscivores are at the top of the aquatic food web and are fish-eating fish, such as bass, pike, and walleye. Piscivores are keystone species, in that their influence may cascade down the food web, affecting other organisms in lower trophic levels. For example, if the piscivore population is too high, they could eat all the planktivores. Without the fish planktivores to eat them, the zooplankton population could increase and do a better job feeding on the algae. This would lead to an increase in lake transparency. The reverse effect can happen if too few piscivores exist, which may be a result of overfishing or poor reproduction.

Microbes in Lakes and Streams

Many sights and sounds attract people to the water, from the waves lapping at the shore of a lake, to the fish and turtles that break the surface now and again. But other components of the fresh-water ecosystem cannot be seen with the naked eye: the microorganisms, or microbes, that constitute the foundation of the aquatic abundance that people see and enjoy. Microbes include bacteria, bacteria-like organisms called archaea, viruses, protozoa, helminths, and protists. Microbes are natural and vital members of all aquatic communities, and are the foundation of lake and stream ecology—without them the natural water worlds would not be possible. Certain microbes, however, when present in excessive numbers, pose a threat to human health.

Ecological Roles of Fresh-water Microbes

Like all ecosystems, fresh-water ecosystems require energy inputs to sustain the organisms within. In lakes and streams, plants and also certain microbes conduct photosynthesis to harvest the Sun's energy. Microbial photosynthesizers include protists (known as algae) and cyanobacteria. Other protists and animals feed on these organisms, forming the next link in the food chain. Plant material from the land also enters lakes and streams at their edges, providing an important nutrient source for many waterbodies.

Decomposers form an especially important part of fresh-water ecosystems because they consume dead bodies of plants, animals, and other microbes. These microbial agents of decay are an important part of the ecosystem because they convert detritus (dead and decaying matter) and organic materials into needed nutrients, such as nitrate, phosphate, and sulfate. Decomposers and other microbes are thus essential to the major biogeochemical cycles by which nutrients are exchanged between the various parts of the ecosystem, both living and nonliving. Without microbial decomposers, minerals and nutrients critical to plant and animal growth would not be made available to support other levels of the fresh-water food chain.

AEROBES AND ANAEROBES

Aerobic decomposers in water need oxygen to survive and do their work. The lapping waves and babbling brook help increase the level of dissolved oxygen that is crucial to so many creatures in lake and stream ecosystems, none more so than the bacteria. If there is not enough oxygen in the water, many parts of the system suffer: the aerobic decomposers cannot digest plant matter, insects cannot develop and mature, and the fish cannot play their part, whether browsing for small food particles or eating other fish. Eventually, the stream or pond will be changed, starting at the microbial level.

Human interaction can jeopardize parts of this system in a variety if ways. One principal way is through the runoff of fertilizers or sewage into a waterbody. Both contain nutrients that plants, algae, and cyanobacteria can use to grow; and excessive nutrient amounts can lead to very rapid growth.

Interconnected sequences of physical, biological, and chemical events may eventually deplete the water's dissolved oxygen supply, leading to changes in the aquatic ecosystem. If the conditions become severe enough, only a few species (known as anaerobes) tolerant of low-oxygen conditions will survive. This process, called cultural eutrophication, can have profound and lasting consequences on the waterbody.

MICROBES AND HUMAN HEALTH

Fresh water is host to numerous microorganisms that affect human health directly. Polluted drinking water is a major source of illness and death throughout the world, particularly in developing countries. In almost all cases, the organisms responsible cycle from the waterbody through the digestive tract of humans or other animals. Released in fecal waste of the infected host, they enter the water again to complete their life cycle. Most infections derived this way cause diarrhea, abdominal cramping, and potentially more serious symptoms, including fever, vomiting, and intestinal bleeding. Some common microbes in lakes and streams that are responsible for disease include:

- The protist *Giardia lamblia*, found in fresh-water bodies throughout the world. Giardia infection is a common waterborne illness in the United States.
- The bacterium *Vibrio cholerae*, while rare in the United States, remains a significant source of disease and death in countries without advanced sewage treatment and with no potable water supplies. For example, a cholera epidemic in 1991 killed more than a thousand people in Peru (South America), where more than 150,000 cases of the illness were confirmed.
- The bacterium *Escherichia coli*, a very common waterborne pollutant. Humans have a large and harmless population of E. coli in their lower, large intestines, and bacteria make up a large fraction of the volume of human feces. When released into drinking water or recreational water sources, E. coli can be ingested and enter the upper

small intestine, causing diarrhea. Other fecal bacteria known as "coliform" bacteria cause similar symptoms. The level of fecal coliform bacteria in pools, ponds, and other waterbodies is frequently measured during the summer months to assess the safety of recreation in these waters.

Treating and Preventing Microbial Pollution

Sewage treatment is the single most important strategy for preventing waterborne microbial pollution. While the earliest treatment techniques simply settled the solids and released the liquids into a much larger waterbody (such as a river or bay), modern sewage treatment relies on multistage facilities that use a sequence of physical, chemical, and biological treatments and filters to treat sewage until it often is cleaner than the original water source from a river, lake, or reservoir.

Hikers and other outdoor enthusiasts can protect themselves by never drinking untreated water from lakes or streams. Water can be made safe in several ways:

- Boiling;
- Filtering (e.g., using small portable filters); and
- Adding chemical tablets, often containing iodine.

Nutrients in Lakes and Streams

When considering the water quality of lakes and streams, two important questions come to mind: "What are nutrients?" And: "Why are nutrients a problem in lakes and streams?"

Nutrients are chemical elements critical to the development of plant and animal life. In healthy lakes and streams, nutrients are needed for the growth of algae that form the base of a complex food web supporting the entire aquatic ecosystem. The most common nutrients in lakes and streams are nitrogen and phosphorus.

Under the right conditions, including abundant nutrients, algae and aquatic plants will continue to grow and multiply well beyond the amount needed to support the food web. The excess growth then dies, and microorganisms break it down, consuming dissolved oxygen from the water in the process. Dissolved oxygen, which aquatic organisms need just as humans need oxygen from the air, can be completely used up by the breakdown process. When this happens, aquatic organisms die from lack of oxygen. Extensive fish kills can result.

Eutrophication and its Impacts

Eutrophication is the process of enrichment of lakes and streams with nutrients, and the associated biological and physical changes. Eutrophication is a natural process, but human activity has dramatically increased its rate in many waterbodies. Lakes and ponds are particularly vulnerable to eutrophication because the nutrients carried into them continue to buildup; in contrast, the nutrients can be carried away in moving water. Some results of excessive eutrophication are visible: thick mats of algae in the water; scum and foam; odor and taste problems; and death and disease of fish and other aquatic organisms. Other effects, such as the reduction in dissolved oxygen, cannot be seen directly, although the conditions often produce visible results such as dead fish.

An increase in the water's pH as a result of the increased growth of algae is another impact that is not directly visible. High pH can be toxic to fish and other organisms, and it can also make other substances, such as ammonia, even more toxic than they are otherwise. Excess nutrients not only affect stream health but also may impact human health and livestock. Although phosphorus is not toxic to human adults in moderate concentrations, high levels of nitrate in drinking water (10 milligrams per liter or greater) can injure or kill livestock or human infants. Nuisance species of algae, such as some cyanobacteria (also called blue-green algae), produce toxins that affect the nervous system and liver, posing a threat to animals and humans who ingest them. The worldwide increase in red tides and other blooms of toxic algae in coastal ocean waters has been linked to nutrient enrichment coming from coastal rivers. Nuisance species such as these, in fresh water as well as coastal oceans, can increase and force out less tolerant species, resulting in a loss of aquatic biodiversity.

Sources of Nutrients

Several sources of nutrients are found in lakes and streams. Some are from natural sources, but many stem from human activities.

Natural Sources

Nutrients are present naturally in lakes and streams, but human activity has greatly increased the amounts going into surface waters. Background levels of nitrogen and phosphorus are generally quite low and are normally measured in milligrams per litre. Background nitrate concentrations in streams are usually less than 0.6 milligrams per litre, whereas background phosphorus rates in streams are even lower, less than 0.1 milligrams per litre. Soil and rocks are the primary natural sources of phosphorus, usually in the form of phosphates. Natural nitrogen sources include leaves and other organic debris from riparian vegetation.

Sewage Treatment Plants

Wastewater (or sewage) treatment plants are point sources of nutrients by virtue of the effluent which they discharge directly to rivers and streams. Unless the effluent has received tertiary treatment, or treatment to remove nutrients, it can be a significant contributor.

In the United States, treatment plants are regulated under the federal Clean Water Act. Under the act, if nutrients are a problem, then more stringent controls can be imposed. Tertiary treatment is expensive, and requires new systems, so some plants spread their effluent on land during times when nutrients could cause water quality problems.

Household Detergents

In the past, household detergents brought high loads of phosphorus to treatment plants, which then were discharged with the effluent. In the United States, however, laws restricting the phosphorus content of detergents have produced markedly reduced phosphate levels.

Septic Systems

Septic systems may contribute large amounts of nutrients, particularly if located close to the water. Standard septic systems do not remove nitrates; however, special systems like sand filters that remove nutrients are now becoming more common.

Sediment

Sediment from excessive erosion is a non-point source that transports phosphorus in particles attached to soil. Construction sites lacking effective erosion control systems can dramatically increase the amount of sediment reaching lakes and streams, bringing in large phosphorus loads.

Animal Manure

Manure is a significant source of nutrient pollution in lakes and streams. Manure from livestock, if not properly managed, can reach streams through runoff or from direct deposits by animals in the water. The U.S. Geological Survey estimates that more than 7 million metric tons (nearly 16 billion pounds) of nitrogen and more than 2 million metric tons (more than 4 billion pounds) of phosphorus are applied to agricultural lands as manure each year. In the same way, pet waste is a nutrient source in urban and suburban areas, and aggregations of ducks, geese, and other waterfowl have also caused problems.

Commercial Fertilizers

Commercial fertilizers are a major source of both phosphorus and nitrogen. According to the U.S. Geological Survey, about 12 million metric tons (26 billion pounds) of nitrogen and two million metric tons (4 billion pounds) of phosphorus are applied annually in commercial fertilizer in the United States. Depending on the composition of the soil in an area, irrigation amounts and application methods, and the amount of rainfall, nutrients not needed by crops either run off the land into lakes and streams, build up in the soil, or seep down into groundwater. Groundwater can seep into a stream and be a source of nutrients.

Atmospheric Nitrogen

Atmospheric nitrogen comprises about 78 percent of the air that humans breathe. The burning of fossil fuels forms oxidized nitrogen compounds, which then reach the Earth when it rains or snows. In some parts of the United States, in particular the Northeast and the Upper Midwest, the so-called "acid rain" associated with these processes conveys large nitrogen loads to lakes and streams. The U.S. Geological Survey estimates that more than 3.5 million metric tons (nearly seven billion pounds) of atmospheric nitrogen are deposited in the United States each year.

5

PLANKTON

INTRODUCTION

Awareness is growing regarding the importance of the oceans and the variety of life they support. Research in many branches of oceanography is discovering the vast unknown of the marine world, and has expanded interest in the understanding of the marine environment and the role each member plays in a complex community. The free-floating organisms known as plankton, from the Greek "wandering," are the drifters of the ocean. Although most of these organisms are motile (moving), they cannot swim or move against currents, but they can move vertically in the water column.

Many marine plankton are found in the deep waters of the outer ocean, or pelagic waters, whereas others are found in the shallow waters known as the neritic zone. Many of the neritic plankton are known as meroplankton, and spend only a brief period of their life cycle in the planktonic category. Many pelagic forms, such as the holoplankton, are planktonic during their entire lifespan. The size of plankton can also determine its general name:

- *Picoplankton:* Smaller than 2 µm; includes bacteria, prochlorophytes, and viruses.
- *Nanoplankton:* 2 to 20 µm; includes diatoms, coccoliths, and silicoflagellates.

- *Microplankton:* 20 to 200 μm; includes large diatoms, dinoflagellates, and small zooplankton, such as ciliates.
- *Macroplankton:* 200 to 2,000 μm; includes large zooplankton, copepods, and invertebrate larvae.
- *Megaplankton:* Larger than 2,000 μm; includes fish larvae and gelatinous zooplankton.

PHYTOPLANKTON

Many kinds of marine and fresh-water organisms utilize inorganic carbon (as carbon dioxide) and fix it into organic compounds by photosynthesis. The principal taxa of microscopic planktonic producers, primary producers, are found over most of the world's oceans, lakes, rivers, and estuaries, and comprise the base of the food web. Phytoplankton consist primarily of diatoms, dinoflagellates, coccolithophorids, silicoflagellates, bacteria, and viruses. All of the organisms discussed below are key players in the microbial food web.

Diatoms have cell walls of silica and pectin, and float in the water column or attach to surfaces as single cells or chains. They are one of the major contributors to primary production in coastal waters, and occur everywhere in the ocean, but are most abundant in colder, nutrient-rich, nearshore waters. Cell division occurs by fission, which is accompanied by a reduction in cell size. They are one of the principal groups that fix carbon through photosynthesis, and this production is prominent during seasonal blooms of short duration.

Dinoflagellates

Dinoflagellates occur as single cells, either naked or within a cellulose cell wall, and many species use flagella to move. These organisms are sometimes classified as protozoa and algae because of their ability to photosynthesize and also absorb nutrients by being parasitic, or by ingesting organic particles. They are second to diatoms in contributing to primary production, and are widespread in the oceans, but are most abundant in nutrient-poor waters offshore. Reproduction is by cell division. Some species are bioluminescent (emitting a pale blue glow seen at night). Dinoflagellates often are the cause of red and brown tides, so named because the algal pigments give the water a colored tint.

Coccolithophorids

Coccolithophorids are single-celled organisms. Many are flagellated, and are protected by ornate calcareous plates, called coccoliths, embedded in a gelatinous sheath that surrounds the cell. These organisms may form cysts that produce spores to produce new individuals. They are most abundant in warm, open-ocean waters, and are sometimes found nearshore. Coccolithophores can photosynthesize (autotrophic) and may also absorb organic matter (heterotrophic).

Silicoflagellates

Silicoflagellates occur as single flagellated cells and typically secrete a silicious outer skeleton. Like coccoliths, these organisms are both autotrophic and heterotrophic, and are most abundant in cold, nutrient-rich waters.

Bacteria

Bacteria are prokaryotes with cell walls made of chitin, and occur as single coccoid cells or long filaments. They often are restricted to waters with low oxygen, and are important in the metabolism of aquatic ecosystems. To support their metabolism, they obtain nutrients by the uptake of organic matter and the release of exoenzymes to lyse (distintegrate or dissolve) particulate organic matter, and attack diatoms, dinoflagellates, and flagellates. Blue-green algae, or cyanobacteria, are photosynthetic. Bacterial activity in marine waters is strongly affected by availability of nutrients and organic matter. Their productivity increases as phytoplankton productivity increases.

Viruses

Viruses play an important role in marine food webs. They infect a wide range of hosts, including bacteria and phytoplankton. They can potentially reduce phytoplankton and bacterial production by viral lysing of their cells and the releasing of dissolved organic carbon. This dissolved carbon can than be utilized by other phytoplankton cells.

Prochlorophytes

Prochlorophytes are a recently discovered group of extremely abundant producers that are barely visible by microscopy. They are most abundant at the lower layers of the illuminated region of the water column, and are now considered to be another major player in primary production.

Nanoflagellates

Nanoflagellates are both autotrophic and heterotrophic. They feed on viruses, bacteria, and some picoplankton and nanoplankton. Nanoflagellates are major consumers of bacteria; some experiments show that they may be able control their abundances when larger predators, such as dinoflagellates, are not present. However, this is less likely to occur in nature.

Protozoans

Nanoplanktonic and microplanktonic protozoan groups are mainly ciliates and heterotrophic dinoflagellates. They consume bacteria, nanoplankton, and microplankton. While these groups engulf their prey, they also release nutrients that stimulate the growth of these same prey.

Zooplankton

Zooplankton are planktonic free-floating animals in fresh and marine aquatic systems, and are the major consumers of the organisms in the microbial food web. These organisms possess a wide range of feeding strategies, from the nematocysts (stinging cells) of cnidarians (e.g., jellyfish) to the complicated mouthparts of copepods. Some are carnivorous (animal-eaters), some are herbivorous (plant-eaters), and some are omnivorous (eaters of plants and animals). These animals can move by means of cilia, flagella, jointed appendages, jet propulsion, or tailed larvae (as in tunicates to larval fish). Reproduction varies from asexual, to fission and fragmentation, to sexual reproduction where some gametes are released into the water and fertilized, yet others are retained and fertilized internally. Zooplankton include many phylum, and not all can be discussed here. Some live their entire life cycle in the water (holoplankton), whereas only the larval stages of fish and other benthic organisms (such as starfish) live in the water column for a short time (meroplankton). All are considered zooplankton. An overview of the major zooplankton phyla follows.

Protozoa

Discussed previously, this group includes ciliates, dinoflagellates, foraminifera, and radiolarian.

Coelenterata (Cnidaria)

Typically known as jellyfish, the major groups are Hydrozoa, Scyphozoa, and Anthozoa. The hydrozoans medusae are the prominent members in zooplankton, and the most common forms are aurelia, pelagia, and siphonophores. These gelatinous animals are major consumers of smaller zooplankton and some of the microbial food web.

Ctenophora

Best known as comb jellies, these possess eight "comb" rows of fused cilia. When they are abundant, these animals can consume phytoplankton and zooplankton, and can clear the water of food for other zooplankton.

Chaetognatha

Known as the arrow worm, this is a common member of deep-water plankton. Smaller species are found in coastal waters, whereas larger species are abundant offshore in blue water. They are predacious carnivores that grasp their prey and paralyze them before ingesting them.

Annelida

This includes many species of marine polychaetes. Many of these organisms can be seen on the surface at night, shedding gametes for sexual reproduction. Their larvae are abundant in the zooplankton community.

Arthropoda

These are the major members of zooplankton and include copepods, shrimp, crabs, lobsters, amphipods, crustaceans, and euphausids, or krill, which are the major source of nutrition for some whales.* The most studied of crustacea are the copepods. These animals are found in all parts of the world's oceans, lakes, and estuaries and are considered the major consumers of most of the organisms in the microbial loop. Because they are holoplankton, spending their entire life in water, they can consume a wide range of food particles, from nanoplankton to microplankton, as they mature. Copepods are responsible for much of the carbon energy transferred from phytoplankton to larger zooplankton.

Chordata

Known as the urochordates (tunicates), this includes ascidians (or sea squirts) and are found on the coast, whereas larvaceans, oikopleura, thaliaceans, salps, and doliolids are pelagic and spend their entire life cycle in the water column. Tunicates are now realized to be major consumers of phytoplankton and smaller zooplankton, and can contribute to the entire food-web dynamics as much or even more than copepods. Larvaceans have retained their notochord and tail as adults and produce a mucus net, or "house," around their bodies to capture food particles. The house is either ingested or abandoned. The salps and doliolids are free-swimming tunicates with a cylindrical or barrel-shaped body with up to eight muscle bands to aid in swimming by jet propulsion and feeding with an internal mucus net. These animals have a complicated life cycle that includes a sexual stage and one or two asexual stages. They are known for their ability to create "blooms," or a rapid increase in their abundance, exceeding 1,000 animals in a cubic meter of water in a short period of time. With this rapid increase in population and their ability to filter feed a wide range of food sizes, they can outcompete copepods during these bloom events. Their role in the food web is being studied more intensely because of their production of large, fast-sinking fecal pellets that can transfer organic matter produced by primary producers to fish and benthic organisms.

Echinodermata

This includes starfish, brittle stars, and sea cucumber. All these animals are meroplankton. Their larvae are a major presence in the zooplankton community.

Mollusca

This includes marine gastropod larvae, pteropods, and cephalopods (commonly known as squid and octopus). Mollusks are consumers of larger zooplankton.

ECOLOGY OF MARINE

Marine ecology describes the interactions of marine species with their biotic (living) and abiotic (nonliving) environments. The biotic environment includes interactions with other living organisms. The abiotic environment includes aspects of the physical habitat, such as water temperature, chemical composition, depth, and current.

Trophic Levels and Biomass Pyramids

The word "trophic" refers to feeding, and "trophic levels" describe the feeding levels in a food chain. The first trophic level includes species known as primary producers. These organisms produce organic material from inorganic substances using resources from the environment and an external source of energy.

Most primary producers are photosynthesizers—that is, they use sunlight as their energy source. Plants and algae are examples of photosynthesizers. Nearly all food chains are based on photosynthesizers, although a few marine food chains depend on bacterial chemosynthesizers, which use a chemical source of energy for production. Chemosynthesizers are discussed later in this entry. The next level in the food chain, the second trophic level, consists of species that eat the producers. These are sometimes referred to as primary consumers or as herbivores (plant-eaters). The third trophic level consists of secondary consumers, which are also called carnivores (animal-eaters). There can be further, higher trophic levels as well. Finally, there are detritivores and decomposers, both of which feed on dead or decaying organic matter. Much of the decomposition work in food chains is done by bacteria.

Species can occupy more than one trophic level, and each trophic level usually has many representatives. Consequently, in most marine ecosystems, trophic interactions are described not by simple chains but as complicated food webs. Many species, including omnivores (eaters of both plants and animals), eat at more than one level of the food web.

Biomass Pyramid

A pyramid of biomass describes the total amount of biomass, or weight of living matter, that is present in each trophic level. The amount of biomass decreases sharply as one moves up from one trophic level to the next (thus the "pyramid"). That is, the total weight of all the producers in a food chain is greater than the total weight of all the primary consumers, which in turn is greater than that of all secondary consumers. This is because not all the energy that a consumer obtains from food is converted to new biomass. For example, the consumer must use energy to catch and eat prey. In addition, a lot of energy is lost to metabolism and heat. In fact, only about 10 per cent of the energy in one trophic level is passed on to the next level. Because of the decreasing amount of energy available in each trophic level, most ecosystems cannot support more than four or five trophic levels.

Phytoplankton and Zooplankton

In nearly all marine ecosystems, photosynthetic species represent the producers at the base of the food chain. Photosynthesis requires sunlight, carbon dioxide, and nutrients such as nitrogen and phosphorus, which are found in sea water. Although there are some photosynthetic rooted plants in shallow marine areas, the majority of photosynthetic organisms in the ocean are microscopic algae, or phytoplankton, that drift along with currents in the water. Phytoplankton are found only in the topmost layer of marine water, known as the epipelagic zone, where there is enough sunlight for photosynthesis. Because of the concentration of producers, many consumer species also are fond close to the water surface.

The amount of phytoplankton in oceans varies across regions and also changes seasonally. For example, phytoplankton are found in low concentrations in tropical waters, where nutrients are in short supply. Phytoplankton density generally is lowest during the winter, when resources are scarce, and greatest during the spring, when levels of sunlight and nutrients increase. Spring often brings algal blooms, or population explosions of phytoplankton. Algae can be so plentiful during the blooms that they color the water, particularly if they contain red, brown, orange, or purple pigments. The amount of phytoplankton available has implications all the way up the food chain, and blooms in algae populations are often followed by increases in populations of other species.

Phytoplankton are consumed by many organisms, including diverse species of zooplankton. Zooplankton are free-floating consumers and include single-celled protozoa, tiny crustaceans, and the larval stages of species such as mollusks and fish. Zooplankton and phytoplankton are consumed by the nekton, free-swimming marine organisms such as fish, marine mammals, and penguins, as well as species on the ocean bottom, including bivalves, crustaceans, and snails.

Examples of Marine Ecosystems

There are numerous types of marine ecosystems. These include coral reefs, tidepools, polar oceans, the abyss, and others.

Coral Reefs

Photosynthetic algae are the producers in coral reefcommunities. The coral reefs represent one of the most diverse marine communities—in fact, a quarter of all marine species are found in or near coral reefs. Photosynthetic algae in coral reefs have a mutualistic relationship with coral, that is, a close association that benefits both members. The algae are sheltered within the corals' calcium carbonate shells and provide nutrients to the corals in exchange. Diverse invertebrates feed on algae and in turn are eaten by reef fish, which are eaten by larger fish species.

Tidal Pools

Tidepool ecosystems are ones that are alternately submerged by water (at high tide) and exposed to air (at low tide). Most of the species found in tidepools are unique to the habitat and are able to survive in both wet and dry conditions. Tidepool food webs, like most marine food webs, are based on algae. Consumer species include bivalves, snails, small fish, and sea anemones. Often the top predators in tidepools are starfish.

Polar Oceans

In polar habitats, such as the oceans around Antarctica and the Arctic, photosynthetic algae also form the basis of the food chain. Algae are eaten by shrimp-like crustaceans called krill, which in turn serve as food for species as diverse as penguins and baleen whales. Penguins are eaten by seals, and penguins and seals are eaten by some whales, particularly killer whales, which are the topmost predators in the system.

Kelp Forests

Kelp forests are marine ecosystems characterized by gigantic species of floating photosynthetic algae called kelp. Kelp can reach lengths of up to 80 metres (about 262 feet). A number of crustaceans feed on kelp, as do sea urchins. These are eaten by larger organisms, such as sea otters.

The Abyss

The deepest part of the ocean, the abyss, extends to depths as great as 6,000 metres (about 19,685 feet, or 3.7 miles). These deep-sea environments are characterized by cold temperatures and lack of light. Consequently, no photosynthesizers exist, although a diverse array of detritivores feed on dead organic matter that floats down from above. There are also numerous predatory and parasitic species.

Hydrothermal Vents

Hydrothermal vents are cracks or openings in the ocean floor where hydrogen sulfide, metals in solution, and other chemical compounds escape into the sea water. Certain specialized chemosynthetic bacteria live in these hot areas and produce organic matter from hydrogen sulfide. They form the base of unusual food webs in this specialized habitat. Chemosynthetic bacteria are eaten by specialized vent worms, clams, and mussels, which in turn provide food for octopuses and other species. The hydrothermal vent crab is at the top of the food chain in vent environments. These unique deep-sea ecosystems are more diverse than most deep-sea environments.

BIOCONCENTRATION

A feature of the ordered structure of food chains is that substances, especially pollutants, become concentrated in large amounts at higher trophic levels. This process is called bioconcentration. Bioconcentration occurs because species that consume pollutants do not excrete them but, rather, store them in bodily tissues, where they accumulate over time. For organisms high in the food chain, their prey organisms have already concentrated pollutants from multiple prey of their own, and so forth. This results in high concentrations of pollutants in species that eat high in the food chain.

An issue of particular relevance in aquatic ecosystems is mercury poisoning. Mercury causes severe health problems in human and other species, including brain damage, and is bioconcentrated in the upper trophic levels. This is why people, pregnant women in particular, are often advised against eating predatory fish such as tuna and swordfish.

6

OCEAN BIOGEOCHEMISTRY

INTRODUCTION

Biogeochemistry is the study of the interactions of the biology, chemistry, and geology of the Earth. In the case of a large body of water such as the ocean, biogeochemistry can be thought of as a huge experiment or set of reactions. Instead of happening in a clean glass beaker, the reactions have the ocean floor as the container. The surface of the water is open to the air, and every day more dust and dirt from land blows over the ocean and falls in. Moreover, the surface of the water contains many small plant forms that are continually growing and being consumed by animals that are themselves consumed by other animals. As this life and death drama continues, the scraps and leftovers drift downward towards the ocean floor like a snowfall; hence the name "marine snow." Around the edges of the ocean, rivers empty water and sediment. Deep in the ocean, mud-dwelling creatures await the arrival of their next meal from the falling biological debris (marine snow). These events are linked to each other, to the history of life on Earth, and to variations in Earth's climate.

CYCLES

Scientists who study biogeochemistry usually consider the cycling of materials through the different parts of the system. To do this, they deal with reservoirs of materials and the fluxes of a substance from one reservoir to another. For example, they examine reservoirs such as the surface ocean water versus the deep ocean water, or the transfer of masses of materials per unit time (fluxes). An example of this kind of approach to biogeochemical cycles in the ocean can be seen in the following figure, where the reservoirs represented are the atmosphere, lithosphere, terrestrial (land-based) biosphere, surface ocean, phytoplankton, and deep ocean. The figure shows the global carbon cycle, a network of interrelated processes that transports carbon between different reservoirs on Earth. Most scientific studies have focused on the carbon cycle. Carbon, after all, is the basis of life on Earth, and its gaseous form, carbon dioxide, is linked to the greenhouse effect and changes in Earth's climate over time. For these reasons, understanding the carbon cycle has been the focus of several large research programmes supported by the U.S. government. Three examples include:

The U.S. Global Change Research Programme (USGCRP): a joint project to design a carbon cycle research programme; funded by the Department of Energy; the National Aeronautic and Space Administration, the National Oceanic and Atmospheric Administration, National Science Foundation, and U.S. Geological Survey;

Global Ocean Ecosystems Dynamics (GLOBEC): a major research programme funded by the National Science Foundation to determine how global change affects the marine ecosystem and what the feedbacks to the physical climate system will be; and

The Global Carbon Programme (GCP): a study funded by the NationalOceanic and Atmospheric Administration to improve scientists' ability to predict the fate of human-derived carbon dioxide and future concentrations of atmospheric carbon dioxide.

Other substances also have well-studied cycles. Water, of course, is constantly moving into, through, and out of the ocean. Some of the atmospheric gases such as oxygen and carbon dioxide are vitally important to life. Nutrient elements such as nitrogen, phosphorus, and silicon are necessary to the phytoplankton, and form the basis for the oceanic food web.

A CYCLING EXAMPLE

The presence of life forms on Earth is tremendously important in the cycling of elements through the major reservoirs. Consider the ocean as an example: If one focuses on the impact of a single diatom on the ocean, the following story emerges. Diatoms are a group of algae living by the millions in each cubic centimeter of surface ocean water. There each alga has access to the sunlight needed for photosynthesis; the CO_2 (carbon dioxide), N (nitrogen), and P (phosphorus) needed to make its soft tissue; the Si (silicon) needed for its shell-like covering; and a number of rare or trace substances in sea water, including Cu (copper) and Fe (iron). To reproduce, it undergoes cell division. Its life processes produce O_2 (oxygen) that can be used by other organisms; organic tissue that becomes food for the next higher creatures in the food web; and often an exudate or slime. Once the diatom has been consumed by an animal (a copepod, for example), its life is over, but its effect on the ocean is not. The copepod digests and derives energy from the diatom's soft tissue, then packages the remains into a fecal pellet that is discharged as waste to become part of the falling debris (marine snow) headed for the ocean floor.

The pellet lands on the ocean floor, forming a site for bacteria to live as well as food for them to consume. The inorganic part of the diatom that remains (the silica shell) will begin to dissolve on the way to the ocean bottom, and Si taken out of the surface water is returned to deeper water as the shell dissolves. Decomposition of sinking organic matter by bacteria returns N, C, and P to the water and removes dissolved O_2.

Carbon

Ocean water itself is changed by life processes. During the growth of diatoms and the consumption of diatoms by zooplankton, carbon is removed from ocean water and in turn from the atmosphere as the diatoms use it to grow. The transfer of this carbon toward the ocean floor and its partial burial in the sediments is often referred to as the carbon pump; it is one of the processes that slow the accumulation of CO_2 in the atmosphere.

Silicon

The silicon (Si) used in the diatom shell enters the ocean from rivers, from the hot springs along mid-ocean ridges and by diffusion from deep-sea sediments. Diatoms remove Si so efficiently from the ocean surface water that it is a very scarce element there, and mixing and upwelling processes are necessary to redistribute enough Si back to the surface to provide for diatom growth. For that reason, Si as well as N, P, and other biologically important elements are in low concentration in surface water of the ocean, and increase with depth, as shown in the figure above.

Oxygen

Another consequence of ocean biogeochemistry can be seen in the distribution of O_2 (oxygen) with depth (see figure above). The oxygen content at the surface is relatively high (about 6 milliliters per liter) and is replenished from the air. Deeper in the water, the O_2 content begins to decrease with depth, until at about 1,000 metres (3,082 feet), the value reaches a minimum. The reason for the decrease is the consumption by bacteria of the rain of organic debris (marine snow) falling through the water. The process requires O_2, and below the surface there is no immediate source to return the O_2 being used up.

The exact amount of O_2 at the O_2 minimum varies with location in the ocean; below the minimum, O_2 content begins to increase again with depth. The increase is related to water circulation in the ocean. The deep water in the ocean starts out at the surface in polar regions, where it becomes very dense because of the extreme cold, and sinks to great depths in the ocean, carrying with it dissolved oxygen from the surface waters. This cold, dense, deep water flows along the ocean floor close to the bottom, well beneath the depths of the O_2 minimum. These factors combine to give the observed shapes of O_2 profiles in the ocean.

HYDROTHERMAL PROCESSES

There are other processes that play a role in determining the nature of the ocean. For example, hydrothermal activity at mid-ocean ridges results in significant changes in the chemistry of ocean water. The water that comes out of these hot springs comes from normal deep-ocean water that runs down into deep cracks on the ocean floor alongside the ridges. As the water penetrates into the oceanic crust, it becomes heated to very high temperatures, and reacts with the rocks. The water that comes out of the vents is very hot; contains sulfide (S^-) instead of sulfate (SO_{42}^-); contains no Mg (magnesium) or O_2 (oxygen); and contains large amounts of Si (silicon). Because the entire volume of the ocean circulates through the mid-ocean ridge system every 10 million years, these changes are of great significance to the oceans and the organisms that live in them.

7

Life in Extreme Water Environment

INTRODUCTION

Beginning in the early 1990s, scientific knowledge of the environmental limits of microbial life on Earth expanded dramatically as microbiologists applied new methods of molecular biology over a broad range of environmental extremes. Microbial species are now known to occupy a vast range of environments that previously were unimagined. New discoveries have revolutionized scientific understanding of Earth's biosphere, opened up new views of the history of terrestrial (land-based) life, and increased the possibilities that life could develop elsewhere in the cosmos. The name applied to this new research area of biology is extremophiles research. Extremophiles (literally "extreme-loving") are defined as organisms that occupy environments judged by human standards as harsh. These encompass both physical and chemical extremes.

Different classes of extremophiles have been defined based on the nature of the environments where they are found. For example, extremophiles that have adapted to high temperatures are called thermophiles. Those that require cold temperatures for growth and reproduction are called psychrophiles (as opposed to other organisms that can tolerate occasional cold temperatures and are not considered extremophiles). Those that love acidic environmentse, with low pH) are called acidophiles, whereas those found in highly alkaline conditions (high pH) are alkaliphiles. Organisms that live under high pressure are called piezophiles, and those found in high-radiation environments are as yet unnamed. Some organisms occupy more than one environmental extreme simultaneously, and are known as polyextremophiles. An example is the archaebacterial species, Sulfolobus acidocalderius, which thrives in boiling mudpots at temperatures exceeding 80° C (176° F) and at acidities less than pH 3. Although mostly microbial, extremophiles include a few species of multicellular organisms such as worms, amphibians, mollusks, and crustaceans.

PHYSICAL EXTREMES

Temperature

Microorganisms are now known to thrive over a broad range of physical extremes in temperature. For high temperatures, this environment includes geysers and hot springs, boiling mudpots, and hydrothermal vents on the deep seafloor. In the latter case, where vent temperature can reach 400°C (752°F), the high hydrostatic pressure prevents vent water from boiling, and thermophilic species exhibit growth up to a temperature of about 114°C (237°F). (Under atmospheric pressure, water boils at 100°C, or 212°F.).

Pressure

Pressure, which is measured relative to atmospheric pressure at sea level (where 1 bar roughly equals 14.5 pounds per square inch), increases with depth in the oceans. In the ocean, this hydrostatic pressure goes up at the rate of approximately one bar per 100 metres. Measured within the crust, lithospheric pressure increases at a rate almost twice hydrostatic. Live microorganisms obtained from the Mariana Trench, the deepest place in the oceans (10.9 kilometres, or 6.8 miles), have been successfully grown under surface conditions, whereas others have been shown to be obligate piezophiles that grow only at high pressure. Pressure decreases with increasing altitude, such that at 10 kilometers (6.2 miles) above the Earth's surface, the pressure is only about one-fourth that at sea level. Organisms have been discovered growing on the top of Mount Everest, the highest point on the Earth's surface (more than 8.8 kilometres [5.4 miles]). Viable spores of bacteria and fungae have even been collected from the lower stratosphere.

Radiation

Radiation is energy that travels as either particles (e.g., highenergy neutrons, protons, electrons, or ions) or waves (e.g., X-rays, gamma rays, or ultraviolet rays). The bacterium Deinococcus radiodurens, which has been found growing on the fuel rods of nuclear reactors, is a famous example of an extremophile that can tolerate high levels of radiation.

CHEMICAL EXTREMES

pH

Chemical extremes in the environment include pH, which ranges from values of less than 0 (extremely acidic) to more than 14 (extremely alkaline or basic). In nature, microorganisms have been shown to occupy nearly the entire range of pH. Some species of bacteria have been found living in a acid mine drainage at a pH of approximately 0.5. Others live in soda lakes, such as those found in the western United States and Egypt, where the highly alkaline waters can reach a pH of 11.

Salinity

Life also occupies an equally broad range of salinity. Salt-loving halophiles live in salt plains, evaporation ponds at saltworks, and natural salt lakes (e.g., the Dead Sea, Israel and the Great Salt Lake, Utah). Halophiles also live within hypersaline brines that exist around deep-sea vents and in deep subsurface rock formations. In nature, salinities can range from fresh water, with very low salinity, to super-saturated brines. At very high concentrations, salt precipitates, often entrapping microorganisms.

Desiccation

The ability to survive desiccation (extreme drying) has been demonstrated for both vegetative cells and reproductive spores of many microbial species. In the driest deserts on Earth, microbial species (so-called "endoliths") often survive by living inside porous rocks where they are protected from ultraviolet radiation. The coldest desert environments on Earth are found in the dry valleys of Antarctica. These polar deserts harbor many types of endolithic communities dominated by cyanobacteria, algae, and fungi. Antarctic endoliths live just a few millimeters beneath rock surfaces in limestones or in translucent, quartz-rich sandstones. Decades may pass with no rain, but when it comes, these organisms spring to life, using the available light, water, and nutrients to quickly grow and reproduce before drying out and again becoming dormant (inactive).

APHOTIC AND ANOXIC ENVIRONMENTS

Even though photosynthesis accounts for more than 99 per cent of the energy that powers the biosphere, thermal and chemical energy sources within the Earth can provide forms of energy capable of supporting complex ecosystems. Consequently, extremophiles can also be found in aphotic (non-light) environments, such as deep in the ocean or in the Earth's subsurface.

In hydrothermal vent environments on the ocean floor, complex ecosystems have been found in which the organisms (including large, multicellular animals) derive their energy entirely from chemical sources provided by the hot fluids issuing from the vent. Single-celled forms of life also survive and grow in the deep subsurface of Earth, within the tiny pore spaces and fractures of endurated rock. These are aphotic environments where sunlight does not penetrate; consequently, organisms living there must use chemical energy sources for their metabolism. Some subsurface microbes do depend on photosynthetically-derived organic matter that washes down from the surface, but many so-called lithoautotrophic species (which literally means "self-feeding from rocks") use simple byproducts of chemical weathering of rocks to extract energy from the environment. For example, oxidation reactions associated with the weathering of basalts in an oxygen-free environment may lead to the release of hydrogen. The hydrogen released is used by methanogens to produce methane and energy.

Although some scientists have questioned the evidence for hydrogenbased microbial ecosystems in deep basalt formations, the possibility of an active microbial community at great depths could have implications for subsurface storage of highly radioactive materials and other wastes. Microbial interactions could act to weaken containers, leading to leakage and the undesirable spreading of waste materials.

Methanogens are microbes that live in anoxic (non-oxygen) environments, which can include some swamps, rice paddies, or certain highly enriched lakes, ponds, or streams, and their sediments. Methanogens combine carbon dioxide (CO_2) and hydrogen (H_2) to produce organic matter, while releasing methane gas as a byproduct. Wetlands and rice paddies (agricultural wetlands) account for half the total methane produced globally. Methane is a greenhouse gas, and its rate of increase in the atmosphere is exceeding that of CO_2. Human activity has played a major role in this methane increase.

Implications and Benefits

The ability of some extremophiles to survive harsh conditions similar to those found on other planets has raised the possibility that life might exist beyond Earth. As an example of this survival ability, halophiles have been cultivated from inclusions of brine contained in salt crystals deposited hundreds of millions of years ago. Microbes also have been isolated from Siberian permafrost, where they have remained in deep freeze for more than three million years. Equally impressive are bacteria germinated from spores preserved in Dominican amber dated at more than 30 million years old. Given the propensity for prolonged survival in these types of environments, could an extraterrestrial biota someday be discovered within brines, salts, or ices on another planet, like Mars or a moon like Europa?

Cellular enzymes extracted from extremophiles have spawned a multi-billion dollar biotechnology industry. The enzymes are used in industrial and medical applications, ranging from the production of stone-washed jeans, to creating artificial sweeteners, to genetic fingerprinting. One thermophile that lives in hot springs is the source of the heat-stable deoxyribonucleic acid (DNA) polymerase enzyme used in polymerase chain reaction (PCR). The PCR forms part of the foundation of much of the biotechnology industry. Proteins produced by psychrophilic organisms may one day prove useful in coldfood preparation and in detergents for washing in cold water.

8

WATER AND THE POTENTIAL FOR EXTRA TERRESTRIAL LIFE

INTRODUCTION

Astrobiology is a new interdisciplinary science that seeks to understand the origin, evolution, distribution, and future of life in the universe. As a fundamental requirement of living systems, water holds a special place in the conceptual framework of astrobiology. All of life's processes are carried out in the presence of liquid water, and on this basis it may be regarded as a key indicator for potential habitability. The importance of liquid water as an organizing principle in the exploration for extraterrestrial life often is articulated in the simple expression "follow the water."

WATER AND PLANETARY HABITABILITY

Most of water's unique properties (e.g., its excellent solvent properties, broad temperature range over which it remains liquid, high heat capacity, and surface tension) are rooted in the ability of water molecules to form hydrogen bonds with each other. In addition, on freezing, there is a slight expansion of hydrogen bond angles that produces a solid phase (ice) of lower density than the liquid phase. This uncommon property results in waterbodies that freeze from the top downward, an important factor for sustaining habitability in polar and other cold climates. Clearly, a knowledge of the past and present distribution of water in the solar system is regarded as crucial for evaluating the potential of other planets (or their moons) to develop and sustain life. Water also holds central importance in the human exploration of the solar system, being essential for the colonization of other planets, such as Mars.

GLOBAL CYCLES

Throughout Earth's history, water has played a central role in the global cycles that link the solid earth and the atmosphere. Interactions between crustal rocks and water sustain a broad range of processes that collectively meet most of the important energy and resource requirements of living systems. Such interactions ultimately determine the overall habitability of a planet, thus setting the stage for life's origin and ensuring its persistence over geologic timescales. The hydrologic cycle (the cycling of water between the atmosphere and oceans) drives a vast transport system that constantly redistributes materials and energy within the Earth's crust. Flowing water and ice transport rock fragments and associated weathering products from source areas to basins of deposition.

Streams and groundwater (inclusive of hydrothermal systems) dissolve, transport, and concentrate chemical compounds required by organisms. Sediments and the dissolved materials formed during weathering processes ultimately reach the ocean basins, where they accumulate as dissolved salts or seafloor sediments. Over the long term, even the dissolved load of streams eventually precipitate out of solution as secondary minerals (such as sedimentary cements) and chemical sediments (such as evaporites). The deposits so formed often preserve signals for environmental change on Earth along with a fossil record of life's evolution.

Over longer spans of time, cycling of the crust by the subduction of lithospheric plates and melting of sediment-covered seafloor and entrapped sea water produce magmas (molten rock materials). The water dissolved in these magmas actually lowers their density and crystallization temperature, thus promoting their buoyant rise back to the surface, where they drive volcanic activity.

OUTGASSING

Over geologic timescales, volcanic outgassing of the Earth's interior regulates atmospheric composition and evolution. The earth's close orbital distance from the Sun ensures a vast supply of solar energy that is utilized by photosynthetically based surface ecosystems. However, the energy output of the Sun was probably much lower (30 percent less than present luminosity) at the beginning of solar system history.

Under these relatively faint young-Sun conditions, an atmospheric greenhouse, sustained by carbon dioxide (CO_2) and/or methane (CH_4), was required to maintain habitable surface conditions. An active plate tectonic cycle over the entire history of Earth has allowed for the constant renewal of the atmosphere by volcanic outgassing. This atmospheric renewal is essential for long-term sustainability. (By contrast, see the discussion of Mars farther ahead in this entry and elsewhere in the encyclopedia.)

By approximately 2.5 billion years ago, interactions between the global hydrologic system and geologic cycles of the solid earth (via processes such as plate tectonics, weathering and erosion, and volcanism) had produced a clear compositional differentiation of the Earth's habitable surface environments into two broad habitats: the continental land masses and the ocean basins. Around the same time, oxygenic photosynthesis emerged as a major biological innovation, taking advantage of the abundant energy available from the Sun. Oxygen production through photosynthesis eventually outstripped volcanic and weathering controls on atmospheric composition, producing an oxidizing surface environment.

By approximately 600 million years ago, the buildup of oxygen in the atmosphere culminated in the appearance of large, multicellular life forms. This new level of organisation in the biosphere enhanced global biodiversity, leading in stepwise fashion to the emergence of terrestrial (land-based) faunas and eventually to intelligent life characterized by self-awareness and advanced cultural, social, and technological civilizations.

EXPLORING FOR MARTIAN LIFE

Given the terrestrial experience of humans, it is easy to understand why the search for water in all its forms, past or present, has emerged as the primary theme for exploration of the solar system. For example, over the next decade, scientific efforts to explore for water on Mars will create a context for assessing planetary habitability and the potential for Mars having developed life at some time in its history.

Presently, the surface of Mars is properly regarded as a radiation-rich frozen desert that is hostile to life. Within about 1 billion years of its origin, Mars appears to have lost most of its atmosphere and, with that, the potential for sustaining liquid water environments at the surface. Interestingly, this early loss of the atmosphere appears to have been the result of the absence of a plate tectonic cycle on Mars.

Yet Mars has not always been a dry, hostile place. Exploration efforts in the late twentieth century revealed that prior to the loss of its atmosphere, Mars probably was much more Earth-like. The ancient southern highlands of Mars harbor a wide variety of water-carved landforms and layered sedimentary deposits of likely aqueous origin. The broad temporal distribution of these features suggests that even though the surface of Mars has been dry for most of the planet's history, liquid water has been present from time to time, providing brief intervals of surface habitability.

Loss of the Martian atmosphere would have spelled doom for any surface life existing at the time. However, if Martian life forms colonized surface environments during earlier wet periods, they are quite likely to have left behind a fossil record. The search for this fossil record is in many ways the focus of the current Mars exploration programme.

The possibility of living Martian life-forms is one facet of ongoing research. On Earth, scientists have discovered that life occupies an incredible range of environmental extremes, including the deep subsurface, where it utilizes chemical energy instead of sunlight. Models suggest that liquid water (perhaps saline) environments could still exist today in the deep subsurface of Mars, along with energy-containing compounds such as methane, which could sustain chemically based life. The argument for subsurface habitability is strengthened by the existence of ancient out-flood channels, believed to have been formed by catastrophic releases of subsurface water in the past. These landforms provide direct evidence that a groundwater system once existed.

But what about today? Scientists recently discovered what appear to be water-carved gullies on the steep slopes and high latitudes of Mars. Despite the constant subfreezing temperatures at those latitudes, water, in the form of subsurface hydrothermal brines, may have risen from deep crustal sources along faults, flowing briefly over the surface and carving the channels.

The origin of these seep features remains controversial, but the hydrologic interpretation is consistent with a variety of other types of evidence that suggest the presence of a subsurface groundwater system. Further investigation of these features is warranted. If a subsurface groundwater system does exist on Mars, such environments may have provided stable habitats for life over the entire history of the planet. In 2002, the gamma-ray spectrometer onboard NASA's Odyssey orbiter discovered extensive water present as ground ice in surface soils over extensive regions of Mars at high latitudes. This has strengthened the case for an abundance of subsurface crustal water on Mars.

Research Challenges

In exploring for Martian groundwater, the practical problem faced by NASA (National Aeronautics and Space Administration) is accessibility. Accessing and sampling sources of subsurface Martian water (and potentially life) will require the development of precision landing systems capable of safely landing on steep slopes where potential seep sites are located, and/or long-ranging rovers capable of traveling to prospective groundwater sites (such as seeps) from safe landing sites located at a distance of perhaps tens of kilometers. Next, scientists will need to drill tó depths of tens to hundreds of meters from small robotic platforms, a capability they presently lack.

Although the previously mentioned technological capabilities have all been identified as long-term goals of NASA's Mars exploration programme, scientists presently lack the technologies needed to access subsurface water on Mars with robotic platforms. As a result, some have suggested that drilling for Martian groundwater may require a human presence, something that is beyond the scope of the present Mars programme. The earliest human missions to Mars, if they can be safely carried out, are unlikely to occur prior to 2025.

VOLCANOES AND WATER

A volcano is a place on the earth from which magma and gases associated with magma flow through the earth's crust onto the surface, whether on land, in shallow waters along the shoreline, or under the sea. Scientists estimate that there are tens of thousands of active and dormant volcanoes on Earth, and thousands more extinct volcanoes. Water and volcanoes are closely linked. Water plays significant roles throughout the "life cycle" of magma: from its production deep within the Earth, to its fiery escape at a volcano, to its final cooling.

Water Introduction via Plate Tectonics

The making of a volcano requires magma, and the making of magma requires heat. In other words, rock that is deep within the Earth must melt before a volcano can form. Most of the earth's interior, although hot, is solid. From experiments it is known that water decreases the melting point of rock. If water is introduced to regions deep within the Earth, then solid rock there may begin to melt.

Water is introduced into the deep earth when oceanic plates descend beneath continental plates, a process called subduction. Oceanic plates, such as the Juan de Fuca plate off the Oregon and Washington coasts, have thick, water-laden sediments at their surface. When these plates subduct, some of the sediments are dragged deep beneath the continents. As a plate descends, the pressures and temperatures it experiences increase, and the water-laden sediments are baked (metamorphosed) and squeezed into new types of rock. At about 100 kilometers (62 miles) in depth, these metamorphosed sediments are transformed yet again, and during this second metamorphism, water is released from the newly formed metamorphic rock.

The released water immediately vapourizes at these temperatures and pressures, and the vapour rises. As the vapour moves upward, it enters hotter rocks, since the deeper rocks have not had time to warm up to the surrounding temperatures and have cooled somewhat due to energy being removed as rising water vapor. These shallower rocks are so hot (1,300°C or 2,372°F) that they are near their melting points. The presence of the water in its vapor phase causes the melting point to decrease and the rock to melt and absorb the vapor. Thus, 100 kilometers (62 miles) beneath the western parts of Oregon and Washington, magma is forming.

CHARACTERISTICS OF MAGMA

The magma that is produced is less dense than the rock from which it melted. Therefore, once formed, the buoyant magma, full of dissolved water vapor and other gases, will slowly force its way toward the surface. As the magma rises, the pressure from the overlying rock is lessened and the magma loses its ability to hold dissolved water. Bubbles of water vapor and other gases, mainly carbon dioxide, start to form.

Water Vapour in Magma

Gases dissolved in magma behave in the same way as gas dissolved in a bottle of soda pop: when a bottle of pop is opened the pressure on its contents is released, causing gases to come out of solution and froth towards the surface. In the same way, when magma moves towards the surface, water vapor and carbon dioxide come out of solution and form bubbles. The rate at which these bubbles form and rise to the surface is a function of the water content of the magma and its viscosity.

Magma Viscosity

Viscosity can be described as a resistance to flow; for example, honey is more viscous than water because it flows more slowly than water. Viscosity in magma depends on two things: temperature and silica content. The higher the temperature of the magma, the lower the viscosity. The higher the amount of silica (which is present in all magmas), the higher the viscosity due to the ability of the silica to form chains (polymers) that link together and hinder the movement of the magma.

CATEGORIES OF ERUPTION

Variations in water content, temperature, and viscosity lead to markedly different eruptive types of volcanoes. Volcanologists usually define two categories of eruption: non-explosive and explosive.

Non-Explosive

Examples of non-explosive eruptions can be seen on the island of Hawaii. The volcanoes on the Big Island spew lava of low silica content, called basalt. As this low-viscosity magma rises within a volcano to near the surface, water vapour in the form of gas bubbles will quickly come out of solution and cause a brief fountaining effect where bits of lava are spattered around the vent, causing a "spatter cone." When most of the water vapor has come out of solution, the eruption becomes less dramatic and the lava flows rapidly downslope. As the basaltic lava cools and the viscosity increases on its path away from the vent, the remaining water vapor bubbles find it increasingly difficult to rise to the surface of the lava flow. These last bubbles become trapped when the lava becomes solid and their shape is preserved as "vesicles" in the rock.

Explosive

Although fountaining, as described above, may be spectacular, truly explosive eruptions occur with the more viscous magmas (andesite and rhyolite, which have a higher silica content). When the water vapor bubbles try to rise they are impeded by the linkage of silica chains in the magma and can rise only slowly. The rapid change in confining pressure as the magma body rises to the surface causes the dissolved water vapor bubbles to expand and escape explosively. Bubbles that form quickly in a large mass of viscous rhyolitic magma can shatter into a froth of tiny glass-walled bubbles, producing a rock called pumice. (A rock with larger bubbles is called scoria.)

In magmas with a high dissolved gas content, the rapid decompression associated with a quickly rising magma body can cause the gases to expand in a violent upthrust of a dense mixture of hot gas, lava, and rocks. (This phenomenon was seen at the eruption of Washington state's Mount Saint Helens on May 18, 1980.) The mixture of gas and rocks rises quickly in the cool air, forming an eruption column that can rise up to 45 kilometers (28 miles) in height. Sometimes, eruption columns can collapse, producing a pyroclastic flow. Pyroclastic flows have proven to be one of the deadliest features of highly explosive eruptions due to the high speed at which they travel, riding on a cushion of air trapped below the collapsing column. They can engulf surrounding villages in hot, poisonous gases, rock, and ash.

WATER CIRCULATION IN INACTIVE VOLCANOES

When a volcano's eruption ceases, the magma within the underground chamber will remain hot for hundreds or thousands of years. Circulating groundwater that comes into contact with the cooling magma is heated and rises to the surface along rock fractures to form either a thermal spring, fumarole, or geyser. Heated water from some thermal springs—for example, in Iceland, Italy, and New Zealand—are used to heat homes and businesses.

Sometimes deeply circulating hot groundwater dissolves minerals from the cooling magma. The dissolved minerals are then precipitated from the hydrothermal solution and deposited in the openings of the surrounding rock, usually filling cracks and sometimes replacing the rock itself. These deposits tend not to have great vertical extent but are exceedingly mineralrich. Many famous silver and gold deposits of the western United States, such as Comstock, Nevada and Cripple Creek, Colorado are examples of hydrothermal ore deposits.

9

SEA WATER

PHYSICS AND CHEMISTRY

INTRODUCTION

Most people come in contact with the ocean only near its surface, and usually near its edges. In the huge part of the ocean that remains hidden, sea water is salty, cold, dark, and deep. Average salt content in the ocean is 35 grams per kilogram of sea water, composed mostly of six constituents: sodium (Na^+), chloride (Cl^-), sulfate (SO_{42}^{-}), magnesium (Mg_2^{+}), calcium (Ca_2^{+}), and potassium (K^+). These are often referred to as conservative elements, because their ratios to each other remain constant throughout the ocean. It is important to measure salinity of sea water accurately. The salinity and the temperature determine water density (which drives water movement), and concentrations of many elements can be indirectly determined from salinity.

Salinity

In the early twentieth century, salinity was measured by chemically titrating the sample to measure the chloride (Cl^-) ion, then making use of the constant proportions of the major ions to Cl^- to calculate total salinity. In the 1950s and 1960s, it became clear that this procedure and calculation were not satisfactory for the precise measurements needed to distinguish and track different water masses in the oceans. Drying a sample of sea water and weighing the salt residue is not practical because some of the salts tend to decompose and lose weight before all the water has been removed. The index of refraction of light changes with the salinity of a water sample; a handheld optical instrument called a refractometer can be used to find an inexact measure of salinity. By 1960, the salinity of sea water was most often measured by a salinometer, which measures the electrical conductivity of the sample compared to that of a standard. Electrical conductivity, the ability of a substance to conduct electricity, increases for water as the amount of dissolved ions increase. Using the measurement of conductivity it is possible to measure salinity with high precision, so salinity can be determined to ±0.0001.

The conductivity can be measured in situ (without bringing the water to the surface) at the same time temperature and pressure are measured. These measurements give a profile of salinity and temperature versus depth (pressure) and are commonly collected by an instrument package referred to as a CTD (conductivity, temperature, depth). The units by which salinity is expressed have changed as the methods of measurement changed. Salinity can be given as grams (g) of salt per kilogram (kg) of sea water (g/kg), or as parts per thousand (ppt). Titration for Cl^- led to the use of chlorinity units, also expressed as ppt. Sea water of 35 ppt salinity has a 19.4 ppt chlorinity. Salinity is now defined as the ratio of the electrical conductivity of the sample at 15°C and 1 atmosphere of pressure to that of a potassium chloride (KCl) solution containing 32.4356 g KCl in 1 kg of solution. (Atmospheric pressure at sea level is about 14.7 pounds per square inch, termed "1 atmosphere.") The KCl solution is measured at the same temperature and pressure as the sample and gives a conductivity defined to correspond to a practical salinity of 35. Because this is derived from a ratio, it has no units, and is written "salinity is 35."

The above definition was formally established in 1980 by the United Nations Educational, Scientific and Cultural

Organisation (UNESCO) Joint Panel on Oceanographic Tables and Standards, putting an end to decades of debate about the meaning of salinity. Some authors, uncomfortable with a unitless value, use psu (practical salinity units). In practice, a sample of standard sea water with a salinity of 35.000 is used as a shipboard standard to compare conductivities and calibrate the salinometer.

TEMPERATURE AND DENSITY

The temperature of the world's ocean is highly variable over the surface of the ocean, ranging from less than 0°C (32°F) near the poles to more than 29°C (84°F) in the tropics. It is heated from the surface downward by sunlight, but at depth most of the ocean is very cold. Seventy-five percent of the water in the ocean falls within the temperature range of -1 to +6°C (30 to 43°F) and the salinity range of 34 to 35.

Variations in total salinity and in temperature cause variations in the density of sea water. Several factors can cause the salinity to deviate from 35. Addition of river water or rainwater decreases salinity; excess evaporation or formation of pack ice causes salinity to increase (because ice crystals themselves do not contain salt—the salt is expelled to cracks and pores between the crystals).

Cold sea water is denser than warm sea water. There are several areas at the ocean surface where surface water becomes very cold. In these locations, surface sea water becomes denser than the surrounding water and sinks to begin the formation of slow thermohaline currents, which move deep-ocean water.

Density differences among different water masses allow physical oceanographers to calculate movements of water in the ocean. The density of a water sample is a measure of the total mass in a given unit volume. Salinity increases the density because the dissolved salts are contained in the same volume as the water. Water molecules cluster more closely around positive and negative ions in solution in a process called electrostriction, which also serves to increase sea-water density.

Density of water in the ocean, reported as sigma t (st), is calculated from temperature, salinity and pressure by using the equation of state for sea water:st = (s - 1) x 1,000. At 4°C and salinity of 35, the density s of sea water is 1.02781 gram per cubic centimeter, and st = 27.81.

At depth, pressure from the overlying ocean water becomes very high (pressure at 4,000 metres is about 400 atmospheres), but water is only slightly compressible, so that there is only a minor pressure effect on density. At a depth of 4,000 metres, water decreases in volume only by 1.8 per cent. Although the high pressure at depth has only a slight effect on the water, it has a much greater effect on easily compressible materials.

DENSITY STRUCTURE OF THE OCEAN

The light and heat from the Sun can only directly penetrate a short distance into the ocean. The surface water is warmer and thus less dense than deep water, which gives most of the ocean a stable density arrangement. The temperature and density often are relatively constant in the surface zone or mixed layer (upper 100 to 200 metres), and begin to change more abruptly in deeper water. The mixed layer is only about two per cent of the total ocean volume, but covers most of its surface.

Temperature decreases and density increases more abruptly in deeper water; the same structure exists in lakes. Many swimmers will recall the experience of finding cooler water at greater depths in lakes. The zone separating surface ocean water from deep water is the pycnocline, containing 18 percent of ocean volume. The deep zone lies below the pycnocline, and contains 80 per cent of the ocean volume; its temperature and density are much less variable than those found in the pycnocline.

LIGHT AND SOUND IN THE OCEAN

Light most of the ocean lies in complete blackness. Sunlight reaches only depths of about 100 metres (330 feet) in clear open water. This lighted layer is referred to as the photic zone. The depth of light penetration is decreased by particles in the water, including any algal cells that are growing there. Coastal waters with a high sediment content, or water in which an algal bloom is occurring, have much shallower light penetration than clear open-ocean water. Water absorbs different wavelengths of light differently. By a depth of 10 metres (33 feet), mostly blue-green light remains, explaining the bluish color of underwater photos taken in natural light.

Sound

Sound travels at 1,450 metres (4,750 feet) per second in sea water compared to 334 metres (1,100 feet) per second in air. Sound in water is reflected back when it strikes a solid object. Because the speed of sound in water is well known, this behavior is used to measure distances under the ocean; a signal is sent out and the time required for the return of the reflected sound can give an accurate measure of the distance to the object that reflected it. This technique is used to measure the depth of water from the surface to the seafloor under a ship; the PDR (precision depth recorder) uses a narrow sound beam to give a continuous record of the water depth through which the ship is moving.

Some wavelengths of sound can penetrate the seafloor to some degree, and hence show the layering in sediment. Depth recorders can detect the presence of fish below the surface and record the movements of the deep scattering layer, swarms of small organisms that move toward and away from the sea surface as the time of day changes.

Sonar (sound navigation and ranging) uses sound to locate and identify targets such as submarines. Navies have conducted years of research on sound propagation in water. The speed of sound in water increases as temperature, salinity, and depth increase. Differences in these properties in layers of ocean water cause the sound to refract, or bend, as it travels through the ocean. Refraction can easily make the sound appear to come from a different direction than its real source location, so an accurate understanding of sound physics has been vital for naval operations.

A zone of minimum sound velocity exists at a depth of roughly 1,000 meters (about 0.6 mile) called the sofar (sound fixing and ranging) channel. Sound signals that originate in the sofar channel ted to stay in the channel rather than escaping. The sound may travel enormous distances in this channel; explosions set off in the channel in Australia have been heard in Bermuda.

A project called ATOC (Acoustic Thermometry of Ocean Climat) was being tested as of 2002. Its goal is to measure global climate change by observing changes in the speed of sound in the sofar channel that would indicate changes in ocean temperatures. Research to determine the effects of this project on marine mammals also is underway.

CARBON DIOXIDE IN THE OCEAN

Carbo dioxide (CO_2) is considered a trace gas in the atmosphere ecause it is much less abundant than oxygen or nitrogen. However, this trace gas plays a vital role in sustaining life on Eart and in controlling the Earth's climate by trapping heat in the atmosphere.

The oceans play an important role in regulating the amount of CO_2 in the atmosphere because CO_2 can move quickly into and out of the oceans. Once in the oceans, the CO_2 no longer traps heat. CO_2 also moves quickly between the atmosphere and the land biosphere (material that is or was living on land).

Of the three places where carbon is stored—atmosphere, oceans, and land biosphere—approximately 93 per cent of the CO_2 is found in the oceans. The atmosphere, at about 750 petagrams of carbon (a petagram [Pg] is 1015 grams), has the smallest amount of carbon.

Balances in Carbon Dioxide Levels

Approximately 90 to 100 Pg of carbon moves back and forth between the atmosphere and the oceans, and between the atmosphere and the land biosphere. Although these exchange rates are large relative to the total amount of carbon stored in the atmosphere, the concentration of CO_2 was constant at 280 parts per million (ppm) by volume for at least 1,000 years prior to the industrial era. Atmospheric concentrations of CO_2 were constant because the carbon being removed from the atmosphere in some places exactly matched the CO2 being added to the atmosphere in other places.

Today, CO_2 concentrations in the atmosphere are increasing as a direct result of human activities such as deforestation and the burning of fossil fuels (e.g., coal and oil). Over the past 150 years, CO_2 concentrations in the atmosphere have increased by as much as 30 per cent (from 280 to 370 ppm).

All trees, nearly all plants from cold climates, and most agricultural crops respond to increasing atmospheric CO_2 levels by increasing the amount of CO_2 they take up for photosynthesis . It is believed that the increased uptake in land plants from rising atmospheric CO_2 levels roughly counterbalanced the CO_2 released from cutting down tropical rain forests and other agricultural practices in the decade of the 1980s. In the 1990s, the land biosphere was estimated to take up approximately 1 Pg more CO_2 than it released each year.

Most of the CO_2 released from the burning of fossil fuels and other human activities (e.g., cement manufacturing) is stored either in the atmosphere or in the oceans. The CO_2 that remains in the atmosphere acts as a greenhouse gas, absorbing long-wavelength radiation (heat) in the atmosphere. CO_2 taken up by the oceans does not affect the Earth's heat balance, so an understanding of the air-sea exchange of CO_2 is an essential part of understanding the Earth's climate system and the potential impact of future CO_2 emissions.

Regulating Carbon Dioxide Emissions

The potential for anthropogenic (human-derived) CO_2 to adversely affect the Earth's climate has resulted in attempts on the international level to regulate global CO_2 emissions. The Kyoto Protocol, for example, was designed to reduce global

CO_2 emissions to 5 percent below 1990 levels. As of late 2002, the Protocol had not been ratified and global emissions have continued to rise. Global emissions in 2001 were roughly 11 percent higher than 1990 levels.

Natural Ocean Carbon Cycle

The oceans contain about 50 times more CO_2 than the atmosphere and 19 times more than the land biosphere. CO_2 moves between the atmosphere and the ocean by molecular diffusion when there is a difference between CO_2 gas pressure (pCO_2) between the atmosphere and oceans. For example, when the atmospheric pCO_2 is higher than the surface ocean, CO_2 diffuses across the air-sea boundary into the sea water.

The oceans are able to hold much more carbon than the atmosphere because most of the CO_2 that diffuses into the oceans reacts with the water to form carbonic acid and its dissociation products, bicarbonate and carbonate ions . The conversion of CO_2 gas into nongaseous forms such as carbonic acid and bicarbonate and carbonate ions effectively reduces the CO_2 gas pressure in the water, thereby allowing more diffusion from the atmosphere.

The oceans are mixed much more slowly than the atmosphere, so there are large horizontal and vertical changes in CO_2 concentration. In general, tropical waters release CO_2 to the atmosphere, whereas high-latitude oceans take up CO_2 from the atmosphere. CO_2 is also about 10 percent higher in the deep ocean than at the surface. The two basic mechanisms that control the distribution of carbon in the oceans are referred to as the solubility pump and the biological pump.

Solubility Pump

The solubility pump is driven by two principal factors. First, more than twice as much CO_2 can dissolve into cold polar waters than in the warm equatorial waters. As major ocean currents (e.g., the Gulf Stream) move waters from the tropics to the poles, they are cooled and can take up more CO_2 from the atmosphere. Second, the high latitude zones are also places where deep waters are formed. As the waters are cooled, they become denser and sink into the ocean's interior, taking with them the CO_2 accumulated at the surface.

Biological Pump

Another process that moves CO_2 away from the surface ocean is called the biological pump. Growth of marine plants (e.g., phytoplankton) takes CO_2 and other chemicals from sea water to make plant tissue. Microscopic marine animals, called zooplankton, eat the phytoplankton and provide the basis for the food web for all animal life in the sea. Because photosynthesis requires light, phytoplankton only grow in the nearsurface ocean, where sufficient light can penetrate.

Although most of the CO_2 taken up by phytoplankton is recycled near the surface, a substantial fraction, perhaps 30 per cent, sinks into the deeper waters before being converted back into CO_2 by marine bacteria. Only about 0.1 per cent reaches the seafloor to be buried in the sediments.

The CO_2 that is recycled at depth is slowly carried large distances by currents to areas where the waters return to the surface (upwelling regions). When the waters regain contact with the atmosphere, the CO_2 originally taken up by the phytoplankton is returned to the atmosphere. This exchange process helps to control atmospheric CO_2 concentrations over decadal and longer time scales.

Anthropogenic CO_2 Uptake

The constant atmospheric CO_2 concentrations in the centuries prior to the Industrial Revolution suggest that the oceans released a small amount of CO_2 to the atmosphere to balance the carbon input from rivers. Today, this trend is reversed and the oceans must remove CO_2 added to the atmosphere from human activities, known as anthropogenic (humanderived) CO_2. In the 1980s, the oceans removed an estimated 2.0 ± 0.6 Pg of anthropogenic CO_2 each year. Because humans are producing CO_2 at an everincreasing rate, the average ocean removal rate increased to 2.4±0.5 Pg of carbon each year in the 1990s.

The uptake of anthropogenic CO_2 by the oceans is driven by the difference in gas pressure in the atmosphere and in the oceans and by the air–sea transfer velocity. Because the pCO_2 is increasing in the atmosphere, CO_2 moves into the ocean in an attempt to balance the oceanic and atmospheric gas pressures. The mechanisms that control the speed with which the CO_2 gas can move from the atmosphere to the oceans (air–sea transfer velocity) are not well understood today. Recent technological advances are helping scientists to better understand these mechanisms.

The transfer velocity is related to the surface roughness of the ocean and the wind speed. The difference in pCO_2 is related to the amount of carbon that is converted from CO_2 gas to other nongaseous carbon species in the sea water, like bicarbonate and carbonate ions. This so-called "buffer capacity" is what allows the oceans to hold so much carbon.

The relative concentrations of CO_2 (1%), bicarbonate ion (91%) and carbonate ion (8%) control the acidity (pH) of the oceans. Since CO_2 is an acid gas, the uptake of anthropogenic CO_2 uses up carbonate ions and lowers the oceanic pH. The carbonate ion concentration of surface sea water will decrease by an estimated 30 percent with a doubling of atmospheric CO_2 from preindustrial levels (280 to 560 ppm). As the carbonate ion concentration decreases, the buffer capacity of the ocean and its ability to take up CO_2 from the atmosphere is reduced.

Over the long term (millennial timescales), the ocean has the potential to take up approximately 85 percent of the anthropogenic CO_2 that is released to the atmosphere. As long as atmospheric CO_2 concentrations continue to rise, the oceans will continue to take up CO_2. However, this reaction is reversible. If atmospheric CO_2 were to decrease in the future, the oceans will start releasing the accumulated anthropogenic CO2 back out into the atmosphere.

The ultimate storage place for anthropogenic CO_2 must be reactions that bind the CO_2 in a manner that is not easily reversed. Dissolution of calcium carbonate in the oceans, for example, is a long-term storage place for CO_2. As the oceans continue to take up anthropogenic CO_2, it will penetrate deeper into the water column, lowering the pH and making the waters more corrosive to calcium carbonate. The problem is that carbonate dissolution typically occurs in the deep ocean, well removed from the anthropogenic CO_2 taken up in the surface waters. In portions of the North Atlantic and North Pacific Oceans, however, anthropogenic CO_2 may have already penetrated deep enough to influence the dissolution of calcium carbonate in the water column.

Sediment Burial

Burial of plant and animal material into the sediments can also provide long-term storage of anthropogenic CO_2. Interestingly, almost no phytoplankton seem to grow faster in higher CO_2 environments, unlike many land plants. This is because phytoplankton growth in the oceans is generally limited by the availability of light and chemicals other than CO_2, principally nitrogen and phosphorus but also smaller amounts of iron, zinc, and other micronutrients.

One proposed approach for enhancing carbon removal from the atmosphere is to enhance phytoplankton growth by fertilizing specific regions of the ocean with a relatively inexpensive biologically limiting chemical like iron. The hypothesis is that the resulting bloom of oceanic plants would remove CO_2 from the atmosphere then transport that carbon into the deep ocean or sediments, effectively removing it from the short-term budget. The effectiveness of the "iron hypothesis" is being tested with several research efforts attempting to scale up iron fertilization experiments.

Other carbon sequestration approaches, including direct injection of liquefied CO_2 into the deep ocean, are also being examined. Further research is necessary to determine whether any of these techniques will be effective or economically feasible. Implementation of these approaches may depend, in large part, on policy decisions made at national and international levels.

OCEAN CHEMICAL PROCESSES

Why is the sea salty? Sea water contains about 35 grams per kilogram of dissolved salt. The most obvious source for the salt is river water, which can easily be observed weathering rocks (from which the water derives minerals), carrying sediment, and flowing continually into the ocean. Because the water added to the ocean evaporates but the dissolved salts do not, it seems reasonable to suggest that river water brings salt to the ocean.

But a closer look shows that the process must be more complicated the major substances dissolved in river water and ocean water. If sea water is simply concentrated river water, these elements should be present in the same ratios in both types of water. For both water types, the Cl/Cl ratio is 1 because that is the chosen standard of comparison. Notice that the ratio patterns for most components for the two water types are quite different. This pattern means that simple evaporation of water cannot change river water into sea water.

Addition–Removal Processes and Considerations

The composition of sea water is controlled by many different processes, all acting at the same time, and adding and removing substances at different rates. The sum of all the processes, a kinetic (changing) balance, determines sea-water chemistry. When sea water dries up completely, it leaves behind a salt deposit called an evaporite. Evaporites of greatly different ages on Earth all are similar, so scientists reached the conclusion that sea water must have had roughly the same chemistry over hundreds of millions of years.

If this is true, then all the processes affecting sea-water chemistry must be at steady state—that is, operating so that the input of salt equals the output. For a steady-state ocean, it is possible to find out how long a particular element stays in the ocean (i.e., its residence time) before it is removed. The ocean is at steady state for a particular element if that element is added and removed at the same rate.

For example, Na (sodium) is added to the ocean at the rate of about 7.9 x 1012 moles per year (3.4 x 105 tons per year) The whole ocean contains 6.4 x 1020 moles (2.8 x 1013 tons) of Na, and the total amount of Na present divided by the rate of addition gives 80 x 106 years, the residence time of Na. In other words, a sodium atom entering the ocean in river water will stay in the ocean for 80 x 106 years before it is removed from sea water.

Residence Time

The concept of residence time is informative in several ways. Elements with long residence times in the ocean tend to be very soluble in sea water and to be evenly mixed throughout the ocean. Thus, Na, Cl, and other elements have long residence times and are known as conservative elements, occurring in the same ratio to one another throughout the ocean regardless of the total salinity.

Elements with short residence times (such as iron and aluminum) are relatively reactive, or insoluble in sea water; they are easily removed and are unevenly distributed throughout the ocean. This makes sense in comparison with the mixing time for the whole ocean, which is about 1,000 years. An element that remains dissolved for millions of years will have been mixed through the ocean many times over, and hence should be evenly distributed. In contrast, an element with a residence time of only 100 years will not be able to make it around once without being removed.

Estuaries

Rivers add huge amounts of dissolved materials to the ocean each year as well as many tons of soil and rock particles. At the boundary between the land and the sea are estuaries, or bodies of water that are chemical and physical transitions between rivers and oceans. As salinity and pH increase seaward, some dissolved substances, such as Fe (iron), may precipitate to form solids and then remove other dissolved elements, such as Mn (manganese), onto their surfaces. Other elements that arrive in the estuary adsorbed (bound) to river particle surfaces may be desorbed (unbound) by the influence of the higher salt content they encounter in the ocean. The dissolved substances enter the ocean, but as much as 90 per cent of river-borne particles are trapped in the estuary and on the continental shelf.

Aerosols

Particles carried through the air are known as aerosols. They come from a variety of sources. Natural aerosols include sea-spray residues, windblown soil particles, volcanic particles, smoke from forest fires, and particles condensed from natural gases. Anthropogenic (human-derived) aerosols, often considered pollutants, include direct emissions such as from smokestacks and particles from conversion of anthropogenic gases.

Because most of the river-derived sediment load is trapped in estuaries and on the continental shelf, a large fraction of particles reaching the ocean from land consists of aerosols. The global mineral dust source is 100 x 1012 grams per year to 800 x 1012 grams per year [(3.5 x 1012 ounces per year to 28.2 x 1012 ounces per year)], compared to a river discharge of 15.5 x 1015 grams per year [(0.6 x 1015 ounces per year)]. Because most of the continental land mass is in the Northern Hemisphere, most of the natural and human-derived aerosols also are generated in the Northern Hemisphere. The amounts in air vary over time and tend to be concentrated in latitude zones.

Aerosols can be delivered to the ocean as dry fallout or as wet fallout if they are entrained into falling rain; in fact, most of the chloride (Cl^-) and sulfate (SO_{42}^-) in sea water is believed to have come from volcanic gases that were dissolved in rain and delivered to the ocean over Earth's history.

Hydrothermal Processes

Sea water continually reacts with its "container"—the basalt rocks that underlie the ocean. The most intense of these reactions occur in hot springs along mid-ocean ridges. The entire volume of ocean water gradually circulates into the ocean floor, reacts with hot basalt, and returns greatly changed in chemical composition.

In this transit, sea water loses all its O_2 and all its Mg; further, all its SO_{42}^- is stripped of oxygen. At the same time, the water gains Ca, Si, Fe, and Mn. When the hot, altered hydrothermal fluids mix with cold, normal sea water, Fe, Mn, and Si precipitate out in huge plumes that look like smoke: hence the names " black smoker " and " white smoker ". The solids formed in this precipitation remove trace metals (such as Cr, V, Mo, U) from solution. (Trace elements occur at concentrations of less than 1 part per million (ppm), or one milligram per kilogram of water.)

It is difficult to estimate how fast ocean water circulates through the mid-ocean ridge axis areas; a reasonable estimate of once every 10 million years suggests the importance of these reactions in establishing the composition of the ocean.

Biological Processes

Life processes have an important effect on ocean chemistry. Certain surface-dwelling phytoplankton (e.g., coccolithophores and diatoms) remove calcium or silicon from sea water to make calcium carbonate shells or opalline silica shells, respectively. These hard particles eventually fall toward the ocean floor, where they are buried in the sediment and thus removed from sea water for many millions of years. The carbon removed by these same organisms to make their soft tissue becomes food for both higher organisms and for bacteria.

The carbon plus the Sun's energy make up the basic fuel for the biogeochemical cycling of material in the ocean. It may be difficult to imagine how an organism as small as a coccolithophore can affect the Ca content of the whole ocean until one considers the enormous numbers of these phytoplankton that occur in the surface ocean.

In addition to the biological debris that falls through the ocean as discrete particles and fluffy bits of marine snow, many inorganic particles from soils are caught up in the fecal pellets and other biogenic materials. All these particles have surfaces that may adsorb dissolved material from sea water and cause them to be buried in ocean floor sediments, thus removed from the ocean.

Evapouration

Evapouration of isolated bodies of sea water accounts for removal of large amounts of salt from the ocean. Salt deposits occur through the geologic record as layers of gypsum, rock salt, sylvite, and other minerals. These minerals represent dissolved salts that have been removed from sea water by evaporation and are mined for table salt and other uses.

Pore-Water Interactions

Interaction with pore water can affect the chemistry of the ocean. Pore water is sea water that has been trapped between sediment grains. The chemistry of the pore water is susceptible to change by biological processes. For example, bacteria in the sediment consume organic tissue, at the same time using up much or even all the oxygen in the pore water.

In the absence of oxygen (O_2), various members of the bacterial population continue to metabolize their food using other energy sources; common examples are reduction of SO_{42}^- to S^-, reduction of Fe(OH)3 to Fe_2^+, and reduction of Mn_4^+ to Mn_2^+. Changed forms of the elements (such as Mn_2^+) in some cases become soluble and diffuse out of the sediment into the overlying sea water; O_2 diffuses from sea water into the sediment. These processes are slow but continuous, and in the long term affect the chemistry of sea water.

CONCLUSION

Many questions concerning the chemistry of sea water remain unanswered. In recent years, work on the composition of tiny sea-water bubbles included in salt crystals from ancient evaporites suggests that the composition of sea water may have changed over the past 700 million years. The changes amount to about a factor of two for several of the major elements; these observations will lead to much future research on the processes that establish ocean chemistry and their changes over time.

10

Tracers of Ocean-Water Masses

INTRODUCTION

The oceans, atmosphere, continents and cryosphere are part of earth's tightly connected climate system. The ocean's role in the climate system involves the transport, sequestration, and exchange of heat, fresh water, and carbon dioxide (CO_2) between the other components of the system.

When waters descend below the ocean surface, they carry with them dissolved atmospheric gases. The time-dependent tracers in the oceans provide information on which waters have been in contact with the atmosphere on various timescales. They also give information on the ocean circulation and its variability.

The timescale information is needed to understand and to assess the ocean's role in climate change, and its capacity to take up human-derived constituents, such as CO_2 from the atmosphere. Thus, the advantage to using tracers for ocean circulation studies is the added dimension of time: their time history is fairly well-known; they are an integrating quantity; and they provide an independent test for time integration of models and biogeochemical processes.

Tracers serve as a "dye" with which to follow the circulation of ocean waters. Conventional ocean tracers include temperature, salinity, oxygen, and nutrients. Stable isotope tracers, such as oxygen-18 and carbon-13, do not decay. In contrast, other radioactive tracers do decay. The radioactive tracers are naturally occurring, such as the uranium/thorium series and radium, and those produced both naturally and by nuclear bomb tests, such as tritium and carbon-14. The bomb contributions from the latter two are called transient tracers, as are the chlorofluorocarbons (CFCs), because they have been in the atmosphere for only a short time. The designation as transient tracer implies a human-derived source and a non-steady input function.

Tracer Timescales Matched to Ocean Processes

The decision of which tracer to use in an oceanographic application depends on the process involved and its timescale. The conventional ocean tracers and stable isotope tracers have no timescale associated with them; their use would depend solely on the natural process involved. For example, to decipher the fresh-water sources in the waters exiting the Arctic Ocean, salinity and the oxygen-18 isotope would be useful. The oxygen isotope is studied because precipitation and the melting and freezing of ice each has different fractions of the ratio of oxygen-18 to oxygen-16.

The radioactive tracers decay with a known half-life. A half-life is the time it takes half of the concentration to disappear. The half-life is matched to what is known about the timescale of the ocean process. For example, to study upper ocean circulation, which occurs on timescales of the order decades, tritium (half-life of 12.4 years) is useful. To study deep ocean circulation, which occurs on timescales of the order hundreds of years, carbon14 (half-life of 5,500 years) is useful. The transient tracers are used to study ocean processes with timescales of less than decades, because that is how long they have existed. This includes upper ocean process, and circulation near the deep-water source regions.

Deep waters that fill ocean basins form primarily in the high latitudes of the North Atlantic and Southern Ocean (the ocean around Antarctica). There is a close coupling of the surface waters in high latitudes to the deep ocean through the density-driven thermohaline circulation. During the process of deep-water formation, atmospheric constituents such as CFCs and CO_2 are introduced into the newly formed water. After these waters sink, they spread out through the deep oceans. As an example of the spreading of deep water from its source in the high latitude North Atlantic, CFCs are used as a tracer.

THE CHLOROFLUOROCARBONS

The chlorofluorocarbons, (CFCs), are synthetic halogenated methanes. Their chemical structures are as follows: CFC-11 is CCl3F; CFC-12 is CCl2F2; and CFC-113 is CCl2FCClF2. The CFCs have received considerable attention because they are a double-edged environmental sword. They are a greenhouse gas and a threat to the ozone layer. The CFCs are used as coolants in refrigerators and air conditioners, as propellants in aerosol spray cans, and as foaming agents. These chemicals were developed in the mid-twentieth century when no one realized they might cause environmental problems.

When released, CFCs are gases that have two sinks: the atmosphere, and to a lesser extent, the oceans. Most of the CFCs go up into the troposphere, where they remain for decades. In the ocean and in the troposphere, the CFCs pose no problem. However, some escape into the stratosphere, where they are a threat to the ozone layer. Destruction of the ozone layer by CFCs removes the atmosphere's ability to block ultraviolet radiation, and has been correlated with the increased incidence of skin cancers.

Since the recognition of the CFCs as an environmental problem in the 1970s and the signing of the Montreal Protocol in 1987, the use of CFCs has been phased out. The atmospheric concentrations have started to decrease, as shown in the figure to the right. (The curves represent the amount of CFCs released into the atmosphere [Northern Hemisphere] between 1930 and 2000.) This phase-out is an important international step toward correcting the dangerous trend of stratospheric ozone depletion.

CFCs IN THE OCEAN

The CFCs are gases, and like other gases they get into the ocean via air-sea exchange. There is a direct correlation between gas exchange rate and wind speed, and the direction of the gas flux between the air and ocean is from high to low concentration. For CFCs, the atmospheric concentrations greatly exceed those in the ocean. The concentrations of CFCs dissolved in the surface layer of the ocean depends on the solubility, atmospheric concentration, and other physical factors. Therefore, the colder the water the higher the CFC concentration. The solubility is only slightly dependent on the salinity. The compounds CFC-11 and CFC-12 were first measured in the oceans in the late 1970s. Concentrations generally decrease as the ocean depth increases. An exception is the western North Atlantic, where CFCs reach to the ocean bottom, because of the proximity to the deep-water source and short circulation time. One of the main advantages to using CFCs as tracers of ocean circulation is that the time-dependent source function permits the calculation of timescales for these processes. A tracer age is the elapsed time since a water parcel was last exposed to the atmosphere. An estimate of age can be calculated from the CFC-11:CFC-12 ratio of the two compounds measured in the oceans and corrected for their solubility. The atmospheric value of the ratio is compared to the atmospheric source function to determine a corresponding date.

The date is subtracted from the sample collection date to get an age. Because the atmospheric changes in the ratio of CFC-11:CFC-12 have remained unchanged since the mid1970s, application of the ratio age for CFC-11 and CFC-12 is restricted to older waters. In regions where surface waters are converted to deep and bottom waters which then spread into a background of low-tracer water, a tracer ratio age represents that of the youngest component of the mixture. Thus, the tracers, such as CFCs, can be used to define the pathways, timescale, and transport for the spreading of deep water from its source regions.

GASES IN SEA WATER

Gases in sea water reveal the ways in which a variety of physical, chemical, and biological processes interact in the oceans and coastal environments. A series of reactive trace gases found in sea water include methane, carbon monoxide, nitrous oxide, hydrogen sulfide, and hydrogen. These gases are both produced by and consumed by various types of organisms. The marine environment can be a source of these gases to the atmosphere.

Major Gases

Atmospheric gases dissolve in sea water as individual molecules. The table lists the percentage of gases in air and in sea water equilibrated with air. At equilibrium a balance exists so there is no net gas transfer between the two phases.

The percentages for a gas in air and in sea water differ due to each gas's characteristic solubility concentration. Gas solubilities vary with the temperature and salt content of sea water. Excluding water vapour, three gases make up 99.96 percent of air: nitrogen, oxygen, and argon. Compared to nitrogen, there are significantly greater amounts of oxygen and argon dissolved in equilibrated sea water.

Noble Gases

The noble gases helium, neon, argon, krypton, and xenon are chemically unreactive. Their concentrations in sea water result from a number of physical factors. Studies of noble gases in sea water show the importance of a process called air injection. When waves at the sea surface break or form whitecaps, small bubbles of air are forced into the water and can be mixed downward where the hydrostatic pressure causes their gases to dissolve and become supersaturated when compared with their solubility at atmospheric pressure. Surface sea water can be about 104 per cent saturated with atmospheric gases owing to air injection.

Oxygen

Oxygen is a very important gas in the ocean because of its role in biological processes. Marine plants such as phytoplankton, seaweed, and other types of algae produce organic matter from carbon dioxide and nutrients through photosynthesis, the process that produces oxygen. The upper 10 to 50 metres (33 to 164 feet) of the ocean can be highly supersaturated with oxygen owing to photosynthesis.

Photosynthesis by plants is restricted to the upper sunlit areas of the ocean, but organic matter settles from the surface layer to deeper waters where oxygen consumption by animals and bacteria is a major process. The oxygen content of deep ocean waters is renewed by a process called thermohaline circulation. When surface waters either cool or become more saline (salty), their density increases and they sink to greater depths in the ocean where they can spread over vast distances.

On a global scale, these dense waters form in the North Atlantic Ocean near Iceland and Greenland, as well as near Antarctica. The dense waters spread throughout all the oceans over periods of tens and hundreds of years, transporting high oxygen concentrations in the deep sea.

The various processes affecting oxygen in the ocean are evident in its profile from the surface to the seafloor. Surface waters are high in oxygen due to exchange with the atmosphere and to photosynthesis. Oxygen content also is high in deep waters because of thermohaline circulation and the slow rates of oxygen consumption at those depths. The waters with the lowest concentrations of oxygen are often found at middepths of 200 to 2,000 metres (656 to 6,560 feet) beneath the surface in a region known as the oxygen minimum zone.

Oxygen plays a very active role in the chemistry and biology of coastal waters, and its concentration is a major indicator of water quality. In many areas of the world, large quantities of nutrients enter coastal waters from agricultural fertilization and domestic wastes. These nutrients stimulate the rapid growth of phytoplankton. When the organic matter produced from these nutrients settles into the deeper waters of bays and estuaries, its decomposition can deplete the waters of oxygen. The result can be fish kills and the formation of hydrogen sulfide gas (H_2S), which is poisonous to many types of organisms.

SEAFLOOR

This vertical profile of dissolved oxygen in the Pacific Ocean north of Oahu, Hawaii shows the high values in the upper 200 metres due to air–sea exchange and photosynthesis. The oxygen minimum zone is between 600 and 2,200 metres. The high-oxygen waters near the seafloor originated at the sea surface near Antarctica and Iceland about 500 to 800 years ago.

Nitrogen

Nitrogen is an essential nutrient required in the photosynthetic production of organic matter by marine plants. Nitrogen gas in the atmosphere and dissolved in sea water cannot be used, however, by many types of plants. Nitrogen must be converted into forms such as nitrate (NO_3^-) or ammonia (NH_3) before it becomes a useful nutrient for most photosynthetic organisms. While the biological cycling of nitrogen is very important in the ocean, it has only a slight effect on the amount of nitrogen gas in sea water. Nitrogen in ocean waters is within 5 percent of equilibrium with the atmosphere.

11

Respiration in Aquatic Organisms

INTRODUCTION

Most aquatic animals need to obtain O_2 from the surrounding water in order to carry on cellular respiration. As we have seen, the amount of O_2 in water is limited, and both O_2 solubility and demand are correlated with temperature. At most, there is only about 15 mg of O_2 per liter of water. In order to carry out the chemical reactions needed to maintain life and reproduce, aquatic organisms must be able to efficiently extract that 15 mg of O_2 from the water.

The primary method of O_2 transport is simple diffusion. Since all molecules are always in motion (except at 0 K), they will tend to move randomly. If they are highly concentrated in one spot, they will be least likely to move towards that spot, as opposed to moving to any of the other spots in the environment. If you divide a card deck into the red cards and the black cards, and randomly move two cards from each deck into the other, you are more likely to move red cards into the black pile, and black cards into the red pile, than you are to move red cards into the red pile or black cards into the black pile, at least until there are about equal numbers of red and black cards in both piles.

Because the speed with which O_2 molecules move in water at normal temperatures is fixed, we can make some estimates over the distances at which simple diffusion can take place in both water and body fluids; that distance appears to be about 1 mm. If a cell is no more than 1 mm from water with sufficient O_2, then no special adaptations are needed for obtaining O_2. If the O_2 concentration of the water is low, or if the cell is greater than 2mm in diameter, or if the organism is multicellular, with some cells buried inside the body, then special measures are necessary.

Cyclosis can help distribute O2 within a cell, but even it has limits, as we shall see. Consider what happens to a cell as it grows. If we are talking about a spherical cell, its volume grows according to the formula v = 0.5236d3 (d = diameter), while its surface area grows according to the equation a = 3.1416d2. The volume is an index of how many O_2 requiring enzymes are present, the surface area represents the "gateway" through which the O_2 must pass. If the volume increases faster than the surface area - and it does, with the volume increasing by a factor of d_3 and the surface area by only a factor of d_2 - than the cell will soon reach the point where O_2 will not be able to enter the cell fast enough. Similar arguments are used to determine the capacities of rooms with various numbers of doors when writing fire codes.

Thus we see that the problem of respiration in aquatic systems is a combination of the amount of dissolved O_2 present, the distance over which diffusion can take place, and the surface area/volume ratio of the organism to be served. Taken together, these factors suggest that life in water should be restricted to very small organisms where diffusion distances are short and surface/volume ratios are high. The fact that large organisms are common in water suggests that there is a way around these restrictions, and, in fact, a number of methods are employed by large aquatic organisms to obtain enough O_2; we will turn to those solutions next.

Solutions

Obviously, one solution is to avoid the problem altogether. There are two basic mechanisms to avoid the problems of O_2

uptake in aquatic systems mentioned above, and many aquatic organisms use both to some extent. They are to stay small and to have a low metabolic rate. Small size avoids the problems with diffusion distances and surface-volume ratios mentioned above; low metabolic rates decrease the need for O_2. Many aquatic organisms, including most larvae, are small enough that simple diffusion will suffice to supply O_2. Low metabolism is also possible, and, particularly at low temperatures, almost unavoidable for small organisms. Unfortunately, warm conditions will raise metabolism rates, often above levels, which can be matched by O_2 uptake; this, coupled with the decreased solubility of O_2 at higher temperatures, may define upper temperature limits for many aquatic organisms.

Problems with small size include the inability to counter strong currents, susceptibility to predation, decreased utility of predation as an energy source (it's hard to feed on organisms as big as you are; smaller ones are better), and decreased ability to control internal conditions such as osmotic pressure and temperature. Natural selective pressures for larger organisms no doubt played a role in developing some of the other solutions to O_2 uptake in water.

To maintain a high metabolism, or to increase body size, other strategies must come into play. The most obvious is to increase surface area without increasing volume, and there are two basic ways to do this. The first is to alter the shape of the organism. We looked at what happens with spheres, where surface-volume ratios decrease as size (diameter) increases. The same relationship holds for other shapes, but it is somewhat diminished for long, thin shapes. For example, let us consider cubes and rectangular boxes. A cube has its surface area equal to 6*L2, where L is the length of the sides, and its volume is equal to L3. Obviously, when the length exceeds 6 units, the surface/volume ratio will be less than one. For a cube 10 units long, the surface area is 600; the volume is 1,000; and the surface/volume ratio is 0.6. Consider a rectangular box 100 units long by 10 units wide and 1 unit high. Its volume is the product of its length times its width times its height or, in this case, 1,000, the same as our cube. Calculation of the surface area of such a box is a little more involved. There are two sides with an area of 100*10 or 1000; two sides with an area of 100*1 or 100; and two sides with an area of 1*10 or 10. Multiply and add up all the areas and you get a total surface area of 2,220 and a surface/volume ratio of 2.22, well above the value of 0.6 for a cube of the same volume.

Organisms that avoid blocky, compact shapes such as spheres and cubes, and tend towards shapes with at least one dimension greatly elongated maximize surface-volume ratios while maintaining a constant volume. This in turn allows for efficient gas exchange even without some of the additional systems we will mention below, and, as a bonus, has the effect of minimizing diffusion distances. For instance, in our cube and box, a cell at the middle of the cube would have been 5 units from the nearest surface; in the box no cell would be more than 0.5 units from the nearest surface; if the units were mm, then all cells in the box would have been able to receive O_2 by diffusion.

In aquatic systems, many organisms apparently optimize their shape in this way. There are flattened organisms such as the simple Mesozoa and Placozoa, Platyhelminthes, Ulva the sea lettuce, nudibranchs, and others. Many seaweeds and aquatic vascular plants such as Vallisneria have flattened blades or leaves; in fact, the leaves of terrestrial vascular plants are also examples of this phenomenon, although here the surface area is maximized to provide for light capture, not O_2 uptake. Other aquatic forms with large surface areas include the myriad vermiform (wormlike) phyla. Simple gas exchange across the surface of the body, whether the body is spherical or wormlike, is called cutaneous uptake, and it is an important source of O_2 for many organisms, even complex ones with more advanced systems as discussed below.

The other way to maximize surface area without increasing volume is to include numerous small protrusions, evaginations or invaginations on the surface of the body. This approach is also common in nature and found in the gas exchange structures of both terrestrial and aquatic organisms, and also in filtration systems, digestive tracts, and even the surface of the human brain.

Some aquatic organisms can get by simply by having bodies with numerous evaginations or invaginations. Sea anemones and jellyfish, for instance, have large spaces inside their bodies that are continuous with the outside water, and cells adjoining these spaces are thus able to absorb O_2 directly from the water contained there. No specialized structures are needed to move the O_2 around the body, and normal feeding movements circulate the water in the spaces. Most aquatic organisms, however, that rely on either basic body shape, small size, or simple evaginations or invaginations, are limited to a life with low metabolic demands. They will be sluggish, slow moving, and unable to support much in the way of nervous tissue, a notorious consumer of O_2. It has recently been suggested that the dorsal nerve cord of vertebrates evolved in response to the need for high O_2 levels in nervous tissues; the prototypic vertebrate may have been a bottom feeder with the ventral side constantly exposed to anoxic conditions; this would have favored migration of the nervous tissue to the dorsal side.

The evolution of larger, more complicated aquatic organisms capable of high metabolic rates required additional solutions to those already mentioned, although, it should be noted, the basic principles we have already seen provide the basis for the solutions employed by more complex organisms. Many of these organisms employ specialized respiratory structures called gills. Gills are basically areas of the body modified for gas exchange by virtue of being either highly evaginated or highly invaginated. The large surface area allows for rapid gas exchange; the only problem that remains is getting that O_2 to the tissues that need it. For this, many organisms have evolved circulatory systems that pump an internal fluid through the gills to obtain O_2 and then transport the O_2 to metabolizing tissue. Often pigments, probably derived from pigments used in the electron transport chain, are used to carry the O2 in the circulatory fluid, or blood.

The vessels must branch enough to bring the O_2 within diffusion distance of any cell in the body. Most organisms use an open circulatory system, where the blood is confined to vessels only part of the time, usually on the way to the tissues. After reaching the tissues, the blood drains back to the heart via sinuses. In a closed circulatory system the blood is always encased in vessels. The greater the demands placed on the circulatory system, the more likely it is to be a closed system; organisms with advanced nervous systems usually have such a system.

The pigments used to transport O_2 are critical. Hemoglobin is the most familiar; it exists in a number of forms and is found throughout the animal kingdom in such taxa as vertebrates, echinoderms, molluscs, insects, crustaceans, annelids, nematodes, flatworms, and ciliates. Other pigments include hemocyanin, a copper-containing pigment found in molluscs, cephalopods, gastropods, crustaceans, and chelicerates; the iron-containing pigment hemerythrin found in sipunculans, polychaetes, priapulans, and brachiopods; and chlorocruorin, a third iron-containing pigment found in some polychaetes. These pigments generally bind O_2 more strongly when O_2 levels are high (in lungs or gills), and release it when O2 levels are low (in respiring tissues). All of the pigments exhibit the Bohr effect; they bind O_2 more tightly under alkaline conditions and release it more readily under acid conditions. Thus O_2 uptake is further facilitated in the respiratory structures where CO_2 levels are low (and thus alkaline pH), and O_2 release is facilitated at actively respiring tissues where there is excess CO_2 and thus an acid pH. Some organisms, such as the midge Chironomus, use hemoglobin not so much as an O_2 transport molecule as an O_2 storage molecule, much the way myoglobin is used in vertebrate muscles.

Organisms with very high metabolic rates, such as fish, go to even further lengths to optimize O_2 uptake from the water. One of the most elegant adaptations is countercurrent flow. Imagine a gill as a flat plate, with water flowing over the thin surface of the plate from front to back. Along the front edge of the gill is a vein; along the back edge is an artery. Oxygen-poor blood flows into the artery at the back of the plate and flows forward through the capillaries, counter to the current of water flowing back over the gill. Almost immediately, the blood will pick up O_2 from the water, even though the water has already lost some O_2 to the gill as it flowed over it. By the time the blood reaches the vein at the front of the gill the blood is nearly saturated with O_2, yet the O_2 does not leak back to the water because the water is saturated with O_2. If numbers help, try it like this: the water at the front of the gill is 100% saturated, grading to 20% saturated as it reaches the back of the gill. Blood at the back of the gill is 10% saturated, grading to 99% saturated at the front of the gill. At every stage along the way, the blood has less O_2 than the surrounding water, so O_2 always flows into the blood, never out. If the blood flowed with the water current, the blood would at best become 50% saturated, for over 50% it would start losing O_2 to the water. Countercurrent flows are the most efficient way to extract something from a fluid, and we will see them again in the heat-exchange mechanisms of aquatic vertebrates and the digestive systems of many organisms.

Aquatic vertebrates, other than most fish, must surface to use their respiratory organs, which are adapted for O_2 uptake from the air. Many fish in stagnant waters also utilize a highly vascularized portion of their gut (the precursor of the lung) to supplement O_2 uptake from their gills. Common aquarium catfish that regularly rush to the surface are doing this; if you notice them rushing often to the surface you may have a problem with the O_2 level in the water. Amphibians probably obtain as much O_2 through their porous, thin skin as they do from their lungs; in fact, there is a family of salamanders, the Plethodontidae, which do not have lungs at all! Frogs and salamanders can remain submerged for long periods of time in water. Turtles also can remain underwater for extended periods by obtaining O_2 cutaneously, sometimes even pumping water in and out of vascularized regiuptake is sufficient to meet metabolic needs in cold weather, such as when the animals hibernate and metabolic activity is low. Reptiles and amphibians often have ways of shunting blood away from the lungs, which are useless underwater. Diving birds and mamThese adaptations are even present in humans, especially human children, and explain why it is not uncommon for people to survive extended periods underwater in cold water (which slows metabolism).

One last group deserves special mention at this point, primarily because it contradicts many of the statements made so far. It is not a trivial matter, either, because this group is the most successful of the animals, the insects. While most insect larvae utili.ze evaginations of the body surface-gills-to respire in water, aquatic adult insects are much different. All adult insects utilize tracheae, air tubes that branch throughout the body and deliver gaseous O_2 directly to every cell. The tracheae are connected to the outside air through spiracles, holes in the body sometimes equipped with a closable flap. Tracheae are tiny, and, because they are not well ventilated, would not function if they had to deliver O_2 in H_2O– in other words, they must stay relatively dry to function.

How, then, do adult aquatic insects do it, that is, breathe, under H_2O? Basically, they cheat by covering their body with hydrophobic hairs that prevent water from reaching the body or the spiracles. They trap a thin layer of air near the bodies, and thus the tracheae remain full of air also. Oxygen can diffuse into this air space and thus be delivered to the spiracles and tracheae. This arrangement is known as a physical gill or plastron. The problem with this system, which is also used by aquatic spiders, is that as O_2 is used up the bubble shrinks. The bubble can be maintained only in O_2 saturated water; a few tiny beetle species living in cool, fast streams are the only insects that can maintain their bubbles indefinitely. All other insects must surface periodically to replenish their bubbles, and large, actively swimming insects in relatively stagnant waters do so relatively frequently. In fact, for a few species, observations have shown that such surfacing is so regular that experienced naturalists can guesstimate the O_2 content or temperature of a body of water by observing how often certain species surface to replenish their air. Other insects obtain O_2 by extending tubes through the water surface (mosquitoes, water scorpions), or even into aquatic plants. Because insects use a tracheal system to move O_2, this burden is removed from the circulatory system. The circulatory system of insects is thus decidedly crude when compared to such groups as the crustaceans or molluscs with similar metabolic demands. Insects posses an open circulatory system which does not have any O_2 carrying pigments; their circulatory system functions mainly to distribute food and heat.

Finally, in our discussion of respiratory systems we have ignored the problem of CO_2 release. For aquatic organisms, this is rarely a problem since CO_2 readily goes into solution and is carried off in the water. If there is enough surface area for O_2 uptake, there will certainly be enough for CO_2 dispersal. Of more critical importance is the osmoregulatory burden imposed by respiratory systems; every bit of surface area available for gas exchange is a surface that is also open to ion or water exchange; a real problem for organisms which are not isotonic in regards to the surrounding water, and the next subject we will take up.

AQUATIC PLANT

Aquatic plants-also called hydrophytic plants or hydrophytes-are plants that have adapted to living in or on aquatic environments. Because living on or under water surface requires numerous special adaptations, aquatic plants can only grow in water or permanently saturated soil. Aquatic vascular plants can be ferns or angiosperms (from a variety of families, including among the monocots and dicots). Seaweeds are not vascular plants but multicellular marine algae, and therefore not typically included in the category of aquatic plants. As opposed to plants types such as mesophytes and xerophytes, hydrophytes do not have a problem in retaining water due to the abundance of water in its environment. This means the plant has less need to regulate transpiration (indeed, the regulation of transpiration would require more energy than the possible benefits incurred).

CHARACTERISTICS OF HYDROPHYTES

1. A thin cuticle. Cuticles primarily prevent water loss, thus most hydrophytes have no need for cuticles.

2. Stomata that are open most of time because water is abundant and therefore there is no need for it to be retained in the plant. This means that guard cells on the stomata are generally inactive.
3. An increased number of stomata, that can be on either side of leaves.

Some species of buttercup (genus *Ranunculus*) float slightly submerged in water; only the flowers extend above the water. Their leaves and roots are long and thin and almost hair-like; this helps spread the mass of the plant over a wide area, making it more buoyant. Long roots and thin leaves also provide a greater surface area for uptake of mineral solutes and oxygen. Wide flat leaves in water lilies (family *Nymphaeaceae*) help distribute weight over a large area, thus helping them float near surface. Many fish keepers keep aquatic plants in their tanks to control phytoplankton and moss by removing metabolites. Many species of aquatic plant are invasive species in different parts of the world. Aquatic plants make particularly good weeds because they reproduce vegetatively from fragments.

Adaptations

- *Free plants:* In a pond community, they receive more sunlight than submerged plants. They also have to compete with one another for sunlight
- *Submerged plants:* Submerged leaves receive low levels of sunlight because light energy diminishes while passing through a water column.

FLOATING PLANTS

- Have either air spaces trapped in their roots or large air spaces (aerenchyma) to help them float to obtain sunlight.
- Have hair on their leaves to trap air.
- Structural adaptation.

  Duckweed, water cabbage
- Chloroplast found on the top surface of the leaves.

- Upper Surface has a thick, waxy cuticle to repel water and help to keep the stomata open and clear.
- Structural adaptation.

  Water Lily
- Structural material to reach higher points and receive more sunlight;
- Structural adaptation;

  Floating heart, water lily, yellow pond-lily, water-shield
- Leaves tend to be broader without major lobbing, remain flat on water surface, maximize surface area and make use of full sunlight, chloroplasts found on the top of leaves
- Structural/ behavioral adaptation

  Most Partially-submerged Plants
- Air spaces within the tissues to keep it buoyant so that its leaves can reach the top of the pond, maximizing the amount of sunlight received.
- Structural adaptation.

  Dissected: parrots teather, Horn wort Thread-like: ditch-grass, quill wort
- Highly dissected/divided leaves or thread-like ones, Allows for a bigger surface area (surface to volume – S/V)
- Structural adaptation
- Hydrilla
- Elongates rapidly to reach water surface and branches out at water surface, more light can be obtained at water surface
- Structural/behavioural adaptation

Human Nutrition

Many aquatic plants are, or have been, used by humans as a food source. Note that especially in (South-east) Asia edible but uncooked hydrophytes are implicated in the transmission of fasciolopsiasis:

- Wild rice (*Zizania*)
- Water caltrop (*Trapa natans*)
- Chinese water chestnut (*Eleocharis dulcis*)
- Indian Lotus (*Nelumbo nucifera*)
- Water spinach (*Ipomoea aquatica*)
- Watercress (*Rorippa nasturtium-aquaticum*)
- Watermimose, Water mimosa? (*Neptunia natans*)
- Taro (*Colocasia esculenta*)
- Rice (*Oryza*) is originally not an aquatic plant.
- Bullrush, Cattail, (*Typha*)
- Water-pepper (*Polygonum hydropiper*)
- Wasabi (*Wasabia japonica*)
- Totora (*Scirpus californicus*).

12

Fish

INTRODUCTION

Fish are aquatic vertebrate animals that are typically ectothermic (previously cold-blooded), covered with scales, and equipped with two sets of paired fins and several unpaired fins. Fish are abundant in the sea and in fresh water, with species being known from mountain streams (e.g., char and gudgeon) as well as in the deepest depths of the ocean (e.g., gulpers and anglerfish).

Fish are of tremendous importance as food for people around the world, either collected from the wild or farmed in much the same way as cattle or chickens (see Ch 14: Aquaculture). Fish are also exploited for recreation, through angling and fishkeeping, and are commonly exhibited in public aquaria.

Fish have an important role in many cultures through the ages, ranging as widely as deities and religious symbols to subjects of books and popular movies in various cultures.

Definition

The term "fish" is most precisely used to describe any non-tetrapod chordate, (i.e., an animal with a backbone), that has gills throughout life and has limbs, if any, in the shape of fins Unlike groupings such as birds or mammals, fish are not a single clade but a paraphyletic collection of taxa, including hagfishes, lampreys, sharks and rays, ray-finned fishes, coelacanths, and lungfishes.

A typical fish is ectothermic, has a streamlined body that allows it to swim rapidly, extracts oxygen from the water using gills or an accessory breathing organ to enable it to breathe atmospheric oxygen, has two sets of paired fins, usually one or two (rarely three) dorsal fins, an anal fin, and a tail fin, has jaws, has skin that is usually covered with scales, and lays eggs that are fertilized internally or externally.

To each of these there are exceptions. Tuna, swordfish, and some species of sharks show some warm-blooded adaptations, and are able to raise their body temperature significantly above that of the ambient water surrounding them treamlining and swimming performance varies from highly streamlined and rapid swimmers which are able to reach 10-20 body-lengths per second (such as tuna, salmon, and jacks) through to slow but more maneuverable species such as eels and rays that reach no more than 0.5 body-lengths per second. Many groups of freshwater fish extract oxygen from the air as well as from the water using a variety of different structures. Lungfish have paired lungs similar to those of tetrapods, gouramis have a structure called the labyrinth organ that performs a similar function, while many catfish, such as Corydoras extract oxygen via the intestine or stomach. Body shape and the arrangement of the fins is highly variable, covering such seemingly un-fishlike forms as seahorses, pufferfish, anglerfish, and gulpers. Similarly, the surface of the skin may be naked (as in moray eels), or covered with scales of a variety of different types usually defined as placoid (typical of sharks and rays), cosmoid (fossil lungfishes and coelacanths), ganoid (various fossil fishes but also living gars and bichirs, cycloid, and ctenoid (these last two are found on most bony fish. There are even fishes that spend most of their time out of water. Mudskippers feed and interact with one another on mudflats and are only underwater when hiding in their burrows The catfish Phreatobius cisternarum lives in underground, phreatic habitats, and a relative lives in waterlogged leaf litter.

Fish range in size from the 16 m (51 ft) whale shark to the 8 mm (just over ¼ of an inch) long stout infantfish.

Many types of aquatic animals commonly referred to as "fish" are not fish in the sense given above; examples include shellfish, cuttlefish, starfish, crayfish and jellyfish. In earlier times, even biologists did not make a distinction - sixteenth century natural historians classified also seals, whales, amphibians, crocodiles, even hippopotamuses, as well as a host of aquatic invertebrates, as fish. n some contexts, especially in aquaculture, the true fish are referred to as finfish (or fin fish) to distinguish them from these other animals.

CLASSIFICATION

Fish are a paraphyletic group: that is, any clade containing all fish also contains the tetrapods, which are not fish. For this reason, groups such as the "Class Pisces" seen in older reference works are no longer used in formal classifications. Fish are classified into the following major groups:

- Subclass *Pteraspidomorphi* (early jawless fish)
- Class *Thelodonti*
- Class *Anaspida*
- (unranked) *Cephalaspidomorphi* (early jawless fish)
- (unranked) *Hyperoartia*
- *Petromyzontidae* (lampreys)
- Class *Galeaspida*
- Class *Pituriaspida*
- Class *Osteostraci*
- Infraphylum *Gnathostomata* (jawed vertebrates)
- Class *Placodermi* (armoured fishes, extinct)
- Class *Chondrichthyes* (cartilaginous fish)
- Class *Acanthodii* (spiny sharks, extinct)

- Superclass *Osteichthyes* (bony fish)
- Class *Actinopterygii* (ray-finned fish)
- Class *Sarcopterygii* (lobe-finned fish)
- Subclass *Coelacanthimorpha* (coelacanths)
- Subclass *Dipnoi* (lungfish)

Some palaeontologists consider that Conodonta are chordates, and so regard them as primitive fish. For a fuller treatment of classification, see the vertebrate article.

The various fish groups taken together account for more than half of the known vertebrates. There are almost 28,000 known extant species of fish, of which almost 27,000 are bony fish, with the remainder being about 970 sharks, rays, and chimeras and about 108 hagfishes and lampreys. A third of all of these species are contained within the nine largest families; from largest to smallest, these families are Cyprinidae, Gobiidae, Cichlidae, Characidae, Loricariidae, Balitoridae, Serranidae, Labridae, and Scorpaenidae. On the other hand, about 64 families are monotypic, containing only one species. It is predicted that the eventual number of total extant species will be at least 32,500.

ANATOMY

Digestive System

The advent of jaws allowed fish to eat a much wider variety of food, including plants and other organisms. In fish, food is ingested through the mouth and then broken down in the esophagus. When it enters the stomach, the food is further broken down and, in many fish, further processed in fingerlike pouches called pyloric caeca. The pyloric caeca secrete digestive enzymes and absorb nutrients from the digested food. Organs such as the liver and pancreas add enzymes and various digestive chemicals as the food moves through the digestive tract. The intestine completes the process of digestion and nutrient absorption.

Respiratory System

Most fish exchange gases by using gills that are located on either side of the pharynx. Gills are made up of threadlike structures called filaments. Each filament contains a network of capillaries that allow a large surface area for the exchange of oxygen and carbon dioxide. Fish exchange gases by pulling oxygen-rich water through their mouths and pumping it over their gill filaments. The blood in the capillaries flows in the opposite direction to the water, causing counter current exchange. They then push the oxygen-poor water out through openings in the sides of the pharynx. Some fishes, like sharks and lampreys, possess multiple gill openings. However, most fishes have a single gill opening on each side of the body. This opening is hidden beneath a protective bony cover called an operculum. Juvenile bichirs have external gills, a very primitive feature that they hold in common with larval amphibians.

Swim bladder of a Rudd (*Scardinius erythrophthalmus*) Many fish can breathe air. The mechanisms for doing so are varied. The skin of anguillid eels may be used to absorb oxygen. The buccal cavity of the electric eel may be used to breathe air. Catfishes of the families *Loricariidae*, *Callichthyidae*, and *Scoloplacidae* are able to absorb air through their digestive tracts Lungfish and bichirs have paired lungs similar to those of tetrapods and must rise to the surface of the water to gulp fresh air in through the mouth and pass spent air out through the gills. Gar and bowfin have a vascularised swim bladder that is used in the same way. Loaches, trahiras, and many catfish breathe by passing air through the gut. Mudskippers breathe by absorbing oxygen across the skin (similar to what frogs do). A number of fishes have evolved so-called accessory breathing organs that are used to extract oxygen from the air. Labyrinth fish (such as gouramis and bettas) have a labyrinth organ above the gills that performs this function. A few other fish have structures more or less resembling labyrinth organs in form and function, most notably snakeheads, pikeheads, and the Clariidae family of catfish.

Being able to breathe air is primarily of use to fish that inhabit shallow, seasonally variable waters where the oxygen concentration in the water may decline at certain times of the year. At such times, fishes dependent solely on the oxygen in the water, such as perch and cichlids, will quickly suffocate, but air-breathing fish can survive for much longer, in some cases in water that is little more than wet mud. At the most extreme, some of these air-breathing fish are able to survive in damp burrows for weeks after the water has otherwise completely dried up, entering a state of aestivation until the water returns.

Fish can be divided into obligate air breathers and facultative air breathers. Obligate air breathers, such as the African lungfish, must breathe air periodically or they will suffocate. Facultative air breathers, such as the catfish Hypostomus plecostomus, will only breathe air if they need to and will otherwise rely solely on their gills for oxygen if conditions are favourable. Most air breathing fish are not obligate air breathers, as there is an energetic cost in rising to the surface and a fitness cost of being exposed to surface predators.

Circulatory System

Fish have a closed circulatory system with a heart that pumps the blood in a single loop throughout the body. The blood goes from the heart to gills, from the gills to the rest of the body, and then back to the heart. In most fish, the heart consists of four parts: the sinus venosus, the atrium, the ventricle, and the bulbus arteriosus. Despite consisting of four parts, the fish heart is still a two-chambered heart. The sinus venosus is a thin-walled sac that collects blood from the fish's veins before allowing it to flow to the atrium, which is a large muscular chamber. The atrium serves as a one-way compartment for blood to flow into the ventricle. The ventricle is a thick-walled, muscular chamber and it does the actual pumping for the heart. It pumps blood to a large tube called the bulbus arteriosus. At the front end, the bulbus arteriosus connects to a large blood vessel called the aorta, through which blood flows to the fish's gills.

Excretory System

As with many aquatic animals, most fish release their nitrogenous wastes as ammonia. Some of the wastes diffuse through the gills into the surrounding water. Others are removed by the kidneys, excretory organs that filter wastes from the blood. Kidneys help fishes control the amount of ammonia in their bodies. Saltwater fish tend to lose water because of osmosis. In saltwater fish, the kidneys concentrate wastes and return as much water as possible back to the body. The reverse happens in freshwater fish: they tend to gain water continuously. The kidneys of freshwater fish are specially adapted to pump out large amounts of dilute urine. Some fish have specially adapted kidneys that change their function, allowing them to move from freshwater to saltwater.

SENSORY AND NERVOUS SYSTEM

Central Nervous System

Fish typically have quite small brains relative to body size when compared with other vertebrates, typically one-fifteenth the mass of the brain from a similarly sized bird or mammal However, some fish have relatively large brains, most notably mormyrids and sharks, which have brains of about as massive relative to body weight as birds and marsupials. The brain is divided into several regions. At the front are the olfactory lobes, a pair of structure the receive and process signals from the nostrils via the two olfactory nerves. The olfactory lobes are very large in fishes that hunt primarily by smell, such as hagfish, sharks, and catfish. Behind the olfactory lobes is the two-lobed telencephalon, the equivalent structure to the cerebrum in higher vertebrates.

In fishes the telencephalon is concerned mostly with olfaction. Together these structures form the forebrain. Connecting the forebrain to the midbrain is the diencephalon. The diencephalon performs a number of functions associated with hormones and homeostasis. The pineal body lies just above the diencephalon. This structure performs many different functions including detecting light, maintaining circadian rhythms, and controlling colour changes. The midbrain or mesencephalon contains the two optic lobes. These are very large in species that hunt by sight, such as rainbow trout and cichlids. The hindbrain or metencephalon is particularly involved in swimming and balance.

The cerebellum is a single-lobed structure that is usually very large, typically the biggest part of the brain. Hagfish and lampreys have relatively small cerebellums, but at the other extreme the cerebellums of mormyrids are massively developed and apparently involved in their electrical sense. The brain stem or myelencephalon is the most posterior part of the brain. As well as controlling the functions of some of the muscles and body organs, in bony fish at least the brain stem is also concerned with respiration and osmoregulation.

Sense Organs

Most fish possess highly developed sense organs. Nearly all daylight fish have well-developed eyes that have color vision that is at least as good as a human's. Many fish also have specialized cells known as chemoreceptors that are responsible for extraordinary senses of taste and smell. Although they have ears in their heads, many fish may not hear sounds very well. However, most fishes have sensitive receptors that form the lateral line system. The lateral line system allows for many fish to detect gentle currents and vibrations, as well as to sense the motion of other nearby fish and prey. Some fishes such as catfishes and sharks, have organs that detect low levels electric current Other fish, like the electric eel, can produce their own electricity.

In 2003, Scottish scientists at the University of Edinburgh performing research on rainbow trout concluded that fish exhibit behaviors often associated with pain Professor James D. Rose of the University of Wyoming critiqued the study, claiming it was flawed Rose had published his own study a year earlier arguing that fish cannot feel pain as they lack the appropriate neocortex in the brain.

Muscular System

Most fish move by contracting paired sets of muscles on either side of the backbone alternately. These contractions form

S-shaped curves that move down the body of the fish. As each curve reaches the back fin, backward force is created. This backward force, in conjunction with the fins, moves the fish forward. The fish's fins are used like an airplane's stabilizers. Fins also increase the surface area of the tail, allowing for an extra boost in speed. The streamlined body of the fish decreases the amount of friction as they move through water. Since body tissue is denser than water, fish must compensate for the difference or they will sink. Many bony fishes have an internal organ called a swim bladder that adjusts their buoyancy through manipulation of gases.

REPRODUCTIVE SYSTEM

Organs

In most fish species, gonads are paired organs of similar size, which can be partially or totally fused There may also be a range of secondary reproductive organs that help in increasing a fish's fitness.

In terms of spermatogonia distribution, the structure of teleosts testes has two types: in the most common, spermatogonia occur all along the seminiferous tubules, while in Atherinomorph fishes they are confined to the distal portion of these structures. Fishes can present cystic or semi-cystic spermatogenesis in relation to the phase of release of germ cells in cysts to the seminiferous tubules lumen.

Fish ovaries may be of three types: gymnovarian, secondary gymnovarian or cystovarian. In the first type, the oocytes are released directly into the coelomic cavity and then enter the ostium, then through the oviduct and are eliminated. Secondary gymnovarian ovaries shed ova into the coelom and then they go directly into the oviduct. In the third type, the oocytes are conveyed to the exterior through the oviduct. Gymnovaries are the primitive condition found in lungfishes, sturgeons, and bowfins. Cystovaries are the condition that characterizes most of the teleosts, where the ovary lumen has continuity with the oviduct. Secondary gymnovaries are found in salmonids and a few other teleosts.

Oogonia development in teleosts fish varies according to the group, and the determination of oogenesis dynamics allows the understanding of maturation and fertilization processes. Changes in the nucleus, ooplasm, and the surrounding layers characterize the oocyte maturation process.

Postovulatory follicles are structures formed after oocyte release; they do not have endocrine function, present a wide irregular lumen, and are rapidly reabosrbed in a process involving the apoptosis of follicular cells. A degenerative process called follicular atresia reabsorbs vitellogenic oocytes not spawned. This process can also occur, but less frequently, in oocytes in other development stages.

Some fish are hermaphrodites, having testes and ovaries either at different phases in their life cycle or, like hamlets, can be simultaneously male and female.

REPRODUCTIVE METHOD

Over 97% of all known fishes are oviparous that is, the eggs develop outside the mother's body. Examples of oviparous fishes include salmon, goldfish, cichlids, tuna, and eels. In the majority of these species, fertilisation takes place outside the mother's body, with the male and female fish shedding their gametes into the surrounding water. However, a few oviparous fishes practise internal fertilisation, with the male using some sort of intromittent organ to deliver sperm into the genital opening of the female, most notably the oviparous sharks, such as the horn shark, and oviparous rays, such as skates. In these cases, the male is equipped with a pair of modified pelvic fins known as claspers.

The newly-hatched young of oviparous fish are called larvae. They are usually poorly formed, carry a large yolk sac (from which they gain their nutrition) and are very different in appearance to juvenile and adult specimens of their species. The larval period in oviparous fish is relatively short however (usually only several weeks), and larvae rapidly grow and change appearance and structure (a process termed metamorphosis) to resemble juveniles of their species. During this transition larvae use up their yolk sac and must switch from yolk sac nutrition to feeding on zooplankton prey, a process which is dependent on zooplankton prey densities and causes many mortalities in larvae.

Ovoviviparous fish are ones in which the eggs develop inside the mother's body after internal fertilization but receive little or no nutrition from the mother, depending instead on the yolk. Each embryo develops in its own egg. Familiar examples of ovoviviparous fishes include guppies, angel sharks, and coelacanths.

Some species of fish are viviparous. In such species the mother retains the eggs, as in ovoviviparous fishes, but the embryos receive nutrition from the mother in a variety of different ways. Typically, viviparous fishes have a structure analogous to the placenta seen in mammals connecting the mother's blood supply with the that of the embryo. Examples of viviparous fishes of this type include the surf-perches, splitfins, and lemon shark. The embryos of some viviparous fishes exhibit a behaviour known as oophagy where the developing embryos eat eggs produced by the mother. This has been observed primarily among sharks, such as the shortfin mako and porbeagle, but is known for a few bony fish as well, such as the halfbeak Nomorhamphus ebrardti Intrauterine cannibalism is an even more unusual mode of vivipary, where the largest embryos in the uterus will eat their weaker and smaller siblings. This behaviour is also most commonly found among sharks, such as the grey nurse shark, but has also been reported for Nomorhamphus ebrardtii. Aquarists commonly refer to ovoviviparous and viviparous fishes as livebearers.

IMMUNE SYSTEM

Types of immune organs vary between different types of fish In the jawless fish (lampreys and hagfishes), true lymphoid organs are absent. Instead, these fish rely on regions of lymphoid tissue within other organs to produce their immune cells. For example, erythrocytes, macrophages and plasma cells are produced in the anterior kidney (or pronephros) and some areas of the gut (where granulocytes mature) resemble primitive bone marrow in hagfish. Cartilaginous fish (sharks and rays) have a more advanced immune system than the jawless fish. They have three specialized organs that are unique to chondrichthyes; the epigonal organs (lymphoid tissue similar to bone marrow of mammals) that surround the gonads, the Leydig's organ within the walls of their esophagus, and a spiral valve in their intestine. All these organs house typical immune cells (granulocytes, lymphocytes and plasma cells). They also possess an identifiable thymus and a well-developed spleen (their most important immune organ) where various lymphocytes, plasma cells and macrophages develop and are stored. Chondrostean fish (sturgeons, paddlefish and birchirs) possess a major site for the production of granulocytes within a mass that is associated with the meninges (membranes surrounding the central nervous system) and their heart is frequently covered with tissue that contains lymphocytes, reticular cells and a small number of macrophages. The chondrostean kidney is an important hemopoietic organ; where erythrocytes, granulocytes, lymphocytes and macrophages develop. Like chondrostean fish, the major immune tissues of bony fish (or teleostei) include the kidney (especially the anterior kidney), where many different immune cells are housed n addition, teleost fish possess a thymus, spleen and scattered immune areas within mucosal tissues (e.g. in the skin, gills, gut and gonads). Much like the mammalian immune system, teleost erythrocytes, neutrophils and granulocytes are believed to reside in the spleen whereas lymphocytes are the major cell type found in the thymus. Recently, a lymphatic system similar to that described in mammals was described in one species of teleost fish, the zebrafish. Although not confirmed as yet, this system presumably will be where naive (unstimulated) T cells will accumulate while waiting to encounter an antigen.

Evolution

The early fossil record on fish is not very clear. It became a dominant form of sea life and eventually branched to create land vertebrates.

The proliferation was apparently due to the formation of the hinged jaw because jawless fish left very few descendants Lampreys may be a rough representative of pre-jawed fish. The first jaws are found in Placodermi fossils. It is unclear if the advantage of a hinged jaw is greater biting force, respiratory-related, or a combination.

Some speculate that fish may have evolved from a creature similar to a coral-like Sea squirt, whose larvae resemble primitive fish in some key ways. The first ancestors of fish may have kept the larval form into adulthood (as some sea squirts do today), although maybe the reverse of this is case. Candidates for early fish include Agnatha such as Haikouichthys, Myllokunmingia, Pikaia, and Conodonts.

HOMEOTHERMY

Although most fish are exclusively aquatic and ectothermic, there are exceptions to both cases. Fish from a number of different groups have evolved the capacity to live out of the water for extended periods of time. Of these amphibious fish, some such as the mudskipper can live and move about on land for up to several days. Also, certain species of fish maintain elevated body temperatures to varying degrees. Endothermic teleosts (bony fishes) are all in the suborder Scombroidei and include the billfishes, tunas, and one species of "primitive" mackerel (*Gasterochisma melampus*). All sharks in the family Lamnidae – shortfin mako, long fin mako, white, porbeagle, and salmon shark – are known to have the capacity for endothermy, and evidence suggests the trait exists in family Alopiidae (thresher sharks). The degree of endothermy varies from the billfish, which warm only their eyes and brain, to bluefin tuna and porbeagle sharks who maintain body temperatures elevated in excess of 20°C above ambient water temperatures. Endothermy, though metabolically costly, is thought to provide advantages such as increased contractile force of muscles, higher rates of central nervous system processing, and higher rates of digestion.

Diseases

Like other animals, fish can suffer from a wide variety of diseases and parasites. To prevent disease they have a variety of non-specific defences and specific defences. Non-specific defences include the skin and scales, as well as the mucus layer secreted by the epidermis that traps microorganisms and inhibits their growth. Should pathogens breach these defences, fish can develop an inflammatory response that increases the flow of blood to the infected region and delivers the white blood cells that will attempt to destroy the pathogens. Specific defences are specialised responses to particular pathogens recognised by the fish's body, in other words, an immune response In recent years, vaccines have become widely used in aquaculture and also with ornamental fish, for example the vaccines for furunculosis in farmed salmon and koi herpes virus in koi.

Some fish will also take advantage of cleaner fish for removal of external parasites. The best known of these are the Bluestreak cleaner wrasses of the genus Labroides found on coral reefs in the Indian Ocean and Pacific Ocean. These small fish maintain so-called "cleaning stations" where other fish, known as hosts, will congregate and perform specific movements to attract the attention of the cleaner fish. Cleaning behaviours have been observed in a number of other fish groups, including an interesting case between two cichlids of the same genus, Etroplus maculatus, the cleaner fish, and the much larger Etroplus suratensis, the host.

Conservation

As of 2006, the IUCN Red List describes 1173 species of fish as being threatened with extinction. Included on this list are species such as Atlantic cod, Devil's Hole pupfish, coelacanths and great white sharks. Because fish live underwater they are much more difficult to study than terrestrial animals and plants, and information about fish populations is often lacking. However, freshwater fish seem particularly threatened because they often live in relatively small areas. For example, the Devil's Hole pupfish occupies only a single 3 m by 6 m pool.

Overfishing

In the case of edible fishes such as cod and tuna a major threat is overfishing. Where overfishing persists, it eventually causes the collapse of the fish population (known as a "stock") because the population cannot breed fast enough to replace the individuals removed by fishing. One well-studied example of the collapse of a fishery is the Pacific sardine Sadinops sagax caerulues fishery off the coast of California. From a peak in 1937 of 790,000 tonnes the amount of fish landed steadily declined to a mere 24,000 tonnes in 1968, at which point the fishery stopped as no longer economically viable. Such commercial extinction does not mean that the fish itself goes extinct, merely that it can no longer sustain a profitable fishery The main tension between fisheries science and the fishing industry is the need to balance conservation with preserving the livelihoods of fishermen. In places such as Scotland, Newfoundland, and Alaska the fishing industry is a major employer, so governments have a vested interest in finding a balance between conserving fish stocks while maintaining an economic level of commercial fishing On the other hand, scientists and conservations push for increasingly stringent protection for fish stocks, warning that many stocks could be wiped out within fifty years.

HABITAT DESTRUCTION

A key stress on both freshwater and marine ecosystems is habitat degradation including water pollution, the building of dams, removal of water for use by humans, and the introduction of exotic species An example of a fish that has become endangered because of habitat change is the pallid sturgeon, a North American freshwater fish that living in rivers that have all been changed by human activity in a variety of different ways.

Exotic Species

Introduction of exotic species has occurred in a variety of places and for many different reasons. One of the best studied (and most severe) examples was the introduction of

Nile perch into Lake Victoria. Since the 1960s the Nile perch gradually exterminated the 500 species of cichlid fishes found only in this lake and nowhere else. Some species survive now only in captive breeding programmes, but others are probably extinct. Carp, snakeheads, tilapia, European perch, brown trout, rainbow trout, and sea lampreys are other examples of fish that have caused problems by being introduced into alien environments.

Aquarium Collecting

Culture

Among the deities said to take the form of a fish are Ika-Roa of the Polynesians, Dagon of various ancient Semitic peoples, and Matsya of the Dravidas of India. The astrological symbol Pisces is based on a constellation of the same name, but there is also a second fish constellation in the night sky, Piscis Austrinus.

Fish have been used figuratively in many different ways, for example the ichthys used by early Christians to identify themselves, through to the fish as a symbol of fertility among Bengalis Fish have also featured prominently in art and literature, as in movies such as Finding Nemo and books such as *The Old Man and the Sea*. Large fish, particularly sharks, have frequently been the subject of horror movies and thrillers, most notably the novel Jaws, which spawned a series of films of the same name that in turn inspired similar films or parodies such as Shark Tale, Snakehead Terror, and Piranha.

The golden fish (Sanskrit: *Matsya*), represents in the semiotic of *Ashtamangala*, (Buddhist symbolism) the state of fearless suspension in *samsara*, thus perceived as the harmless ocean, referred to as '*Buddha-eyes*' or '*rigpa-sight*'. The fishes symbolises the auspiciousness of all living beings in a state of fearlessness without danger of drowning in the *Samsaric* Ocean of Suffering, and migrating from teaching to teaching freely and spontaneously just as fish swim.

Fish riders is a 1920s poster of the Republic of China.In the following quotation, the two golden fishes are linked with the Ganges and Yamuna, and *nadi*, *prana* and *carp*.

The two fishes originally represented the two main sacred rivers of India - the Ganges and Yamuna. These rivers are associated with the lunar and solar channels which originate in the nostrils and carry the alternating rhythms of breath & *prana*. They have religious significance in Hindu, Jain and Buddhist traditions but also in Christianity who is first signified by the sign of the fish, and especially referring to feeding the multitude in the desert. In the dhamma of Buddha the fish symbolize happiness as they have complete freedom of movement in the water. They represent fertility and abundance. Often drawn in the form of carp which are regarded in the Orient as sacred on account of their elegant beauty, size and life-span The name of the Canadian city of Coquitlam, British Columbia is derived from Kwikwetlem, which means "smell like fish" in the Halkomelem language spoken by the area's original inhabitants.

FISH FARMING

Fish farming is the principal form of aquaculture, while other methods may fall under mariculture. It involves raising fish commercially in tanks or enclosures, usually for food. A facility that releases juvenile fish into the wild for recreational fishing or to supplement a species' natural numbers is generally referred to as a fish hatchery. Fish species raised by fish farms include salmon, catfish, tilapia, cod, carp, trout and others. Increasing demands on wild fisheries by commercial fishing has caused widespread overfishing. Fish farming offers an alternative solution to the increasing market demand for fish and fish protein.

Major Categories of Fish Farms

There are two kinds of aquaculture: extensive aquaculture based on local photosynthetical production and intensive aquaculture, in which the fish are fed with external food supply. The management of these two kinds of aquaculture systems are completely different.

Extensive Aquaculture

Limiting for growth here is the available food supply by natural sources, commonly zooplankton feeding on pelagic algae or benthic animals, such as certain crustaceans and mollusks. Tilapia species filter feed directly on phytoplankton, which makes higher production possible. The photosynthetical production can be increased by fertilizing the pond water with artificial fertilizer mixtures, such as potash, phosphorus, nitrogen and microelements. Because most fish are carnivorous, they occupy a higher place in the trophic chain and therefore only a tiny fraction of primary photosynthetic production (typically 1%) will be converted into harvestable fish. As a result, without additional feeding the fish harvest will not exceed 200 kilograms of fish per hectare per year, equivalent to 1% of the gross photosynthetic production.

A second point of concern is the risk of algal blooms. When temperatures, nutrient supply and available sunlight are optimal for algal growth, algae multiply their biomass at an exponential rate, eventually leading to an exhaustion of available nutrients and a subsequent die-off. The decaying algal biomass will deplete the oxygen in the pond water because it blocks out the sun and pollute it with organic and inorganic solutes (such as ammonium ions), which can (and frequently do) lead to massive loss of fish.

In order to tap all available food sources in the pond, the aquaculturist will choose fish species which occupy different places in the pond ecosystem, e.g., a filter algae feeder such as tilapia, a benthic feeder such as carp or catfish and a zooplankton feeder (various carps) or submerged weeds feeder such as grass carp.

Intensive Aquaculture

Thumbing of a male rainbow trout

In this kinds of systems fish production per unit of surface can be increased at will, as long as sufficient oxygen, fresh water and food are provided. Because of the requirement of sufficient fresh water, a massive water purification system must be integrated in the fish farm. A clever way to achieve this is the combination of hydroponic horticulture and water treatment, see below. The exception to this rule are cages which are placed in a river or sea, which supplements the fish crop with sufficient oxygenated water. Some environmentalists object to this practice.

The cost of inputs per unit of fish weight is higher than in extensive farming, especially because of the high cost of fish food, which must contain a much higher level of protein (up to 60%) than, e.g., cattle food and a balanced amino acid composition as well. This frequently is offset by the lower land costs and the higher productions which can be obtained due to the high level of input control.

Essential here is aeration of the water, as fish need a sufficient oxygen level for growth. This is achieved by bubbling, cascade flow or aqueous oxygen. Catfish, Clarias ssp. can breathe atmospheric air and can tolerate much higher levels of pollutants than, e.g., trout or salmon, which makes aeration and water purification less necessary and makes Clarias species especially suited for intensive fish production. In some Clarias farms about 10% of the water volume can consist of fish biomass.

Especially when fish densities are high, the risk of infections by parasites like fish lice, fungi (*Saprolegnia* sp.), intestinal worms (such as nematodes or trematodes), bacteria (e.g., *Yersinia* sp, *Pseudomonas* sp.), and protozoa (such as *Dinoflagellates*) is much higher than in animal husbandry because of the ease in which pathogens can invade the fish body (e.g. by the gills). The same holds for water pollution or depletion of oxygen in the water, which can ruin a fish crop within minutes. This means, intensive aquaculture requires tight monitoring and a high level of expertise of the fish farmer.

Intensive aquaculture was developed as a source for food fish. Raising ornamental cold water fish (goldfish or koi), although theoretically much more profitable due to the higher income per weight of fish produced, has never been successfully carried out until very recently. The increased incidences of dangerous viral diseases of koi Carp, together with the high value of the fish has led to initiatives in closed system koi breeding and growing in a number of countries. Today there are a few commercially successful intensive koi growing facilities in the U.K., Germany and Israel. Some producers have adapted their intensive systems in an effort to provide consumers with fish that do not carry dormant forms of viruses and diseases.

Specific Types of Fish Farms

Within intensive and extensive aquaculture methods there are numerous specific types of fish farms, each has benefits and applications unique to its design.

Integrated Recycling Systems

One of the largest problems with freshwater aquaculture is that it can use a million gallons of water per acre (about 1 m^3 of water per m^2) each year. Extended water purification systems allow for the reuse (recycling) of local water.

The largest-scale pure fish farms use a system derived (admittedly much refined) from the New Alchemists in the 1970s. Basically, large plastic fish tanks are placed in a greenhouse. A hydroponic bed is placed near, above or between them. When tilapia are raised in the tanks, they are able to eat algae, which naturally grows in the tanks when the tanks are properly fertilized.

The tank water is slowly circulated to the hydroponic beds where the tilapia waste feeds a commercial plant crops. Carefully cultured microorganisms in the hydroponic bed convert ammonia to nitrates, and the plants are fertilized by the nitrates and phosphates. Other wastes are strained out by the hydroponic media, which doubles as an aerated pebble-bed filter. This system, properly tuned, produces more edible protein per unit area than any other. A wide variety of plants can grow well in the hydroponic beds. Most growers concentrate on herbs (e.g. parsley and basil), which command premium prices in small quantities all year long. The most common customers are restaurant wholesalers.

Since the system lives in a greenhouse, it adapts to almost all temperate climates, and may also adapt to tropical climates.

The main environmental impact is discharge of water that must be salted to maintain the fishes' electrolyte balance. Current growers use a variety of proprietary tricks to keep fish healthy, reducing their expenses for salt and waste water discharge permits. Some veterinary authorities speculate that ultraviolet ozone disinfectant systems (widely used for ornamental fish) may play a prominent part in keeping the Tilapia healthy with recirculated water.

Irrigation Ditch or Pond Systems

These use irrigation ditches or farm ponds to raise fish. The basic requirement is to have a ditch or pond that retains water, possibly with an above-ground irrigation system (many irrigation systems use buried pipes with headers. Using this method, one can store one's water allotment in ponds or ditches, usually lined with bentonite clay. In small systems the fish are often fed commercial fish food, and their waste products can help fertilize the fields. In larger ponds, the pond grows water plants and algae as fish food. Some of the most successful ponds grow introduced strains of plants, as well as introduced strains of fish. Control of water quality is crucial. Fertilizing, clarifying and pH control of the water can increase yields substantially, as long as eutrophication is prevented and oxygen levels stay high.Yields can be low if the fish grow ill from electrolyte stress.

Cage System

Fish cages are placed in open water resources to contain and protect fish until they can be harvested. They can be constructed of a wide variety of components. Fish are stocked in cages, artificially fed, and harvested when they reach market size. A few advantages of fish farming with cages are that many types of waters can be used (rivers, lakes, filled quarries, etc.), many types of fishes can be raised, and fish farming can co-exist with sport fishing and other water uses. Cage farming of fishes in open seas is also gaining popularity. Concerns of disease, poaching, poor water quality, etc., lead some to believe that in general, pond systems are easier to manage and simpler to start. Also, past occurrences of cage-failures leading to escapes, have raised concern regarding the culture of non-native fish species in open-water cages. Even though the cage-industry has made numerous technological advances in cage construction in recent years, the concern for escapes remains valid.

Classic Fry Farming

Trout and other sport fish are often raised from eggs to fry or fingerlings and then trucked to streams and released. Normally, the fry are raised in long, shallow concrete tanks, fed with fresh stream water. The fry receive commercial fish food in pellets. While not as efficient as the New Alchemists' method, it is also far simpler, and has been used for many years to stock streams with sport fish. European eel (*Anguilla anguilla*) aquaculturalists procure a limited supply of glass eels, juvenile stages of the European eel which swim north from the Sargasso Sea breeding grounds, for their farms. The European eel is threatened with extinction because of the excessive catch of glass eels by Spanish fishermen and overfishing of adult eels in, e.g., the Dutch, Netherlands. As per 2005, no one has managed to breed the European eel in captivity.

Criticisms

The issue of feeds in fish farming has been a controversial one. Many cultured fishes (tilapia, carp, catfish, many others) require no meat or fish products in their diets. Top-level carnivores (most salmon species) depend on fish feed of which a portion is usually derived from wild caught fish (anchovies, menhaden, etc.). Vegetable-derived proteins have successfully replaced fish meal in feeds for carnivorous fishes, but vegetable-derived oils have not successfully been incorporated into the diets of carnivores.

Secondly, farmed fish are kept in concentrations never seen in the wild (e.g. 50,000 fish in a two-acre area. with each fish occupying less room than the average bathtub. This can cause several forms of pollution. Packed tightly, fish rub against each other and the sides of their cages, damaging their fins and tails and becoming sickened with various diseases and infections.

However, fish tend also to be animals that aggregate into large schools at high density. Most successful aquaculture species are schooling species, which do not have social problems at high density. Aquaculturists tend to feel that operating a rearing system above its design capacity or above the social density limit of the fish will result in decreased growth rate and FCR (food conversion ratio - kg dry feed/kg of fish produced), which will result in increased cost and risk of health problems along with a decrease in profits. Stressing the animals is not desirable, but the concept of and measurement of stress must be viewed from the perspective of the animal using the scientific method.

Such parasites have been shown to have an effect on nearby wild fish. One place that has garnered international media attention is British Columbia's Broughton Archipelago. There, juvenile wild salmon must "run a gauntlet" of large fish farms located off-shore near river outlets before making their way to sea. It is alleged that the farms cause such severe sea lice infestations that one study predicted a 99% collapse in the wild salmon population in another four years This claim, however, has been criticized by numerous scientists who question the correlation between increased fish farming and increases in sea lice infestation among wild salmon.

Because of parasite problems, some aquaculture operators frequently use strong antibiotic drugs to keep the fish alive (but many fish still die prematurely at rates of up to 30%. In some cases, these drugs have entered the environment. Additionally, the residual presence of these drugs in human food products has become controversial. Use of antibiotics in food production is thought to increase the prevalence of antibiotic resistance in human diseases. The use of antibiotic drugs in aquaculture has decreased considerably in the last decade. Vaccinations and other techniques have virtually eliminated the need for antibiotics.

The lice and pathogen problems of the 1990s facilitated the development of current treatment methods for sea lice and pathogens. These developments reduced the stress from parasite/pathogen problems. However, being in an ocean environment, the transfer of disease organisms from the wild fish to the aquaculture fish is an ever-present risk factor.

The very large number of fish kept long-term in a single location produces a significant amount of condensed feces, often contaminated with drugs, which again affect local waterways. However, these effects are very local to the actual fish farm site and are minimal to non-measurable in high current sites.

Other potential problems faced by aquaculturists are the obtaining of various permits and water-use rights, profitability, concerns about invasive species and genetic engineering depending on what species are involved, and interaction with the United Nations Convention on the Law of the Sea.

Environmentally Friendly Methods

An alternative to open ocean cage aquaculture, one in which the risk of environmental damage is substantially eliminated is through the use of a recirculating aquaculture system (RAS). A RAS is a series of culture tanks and filters where water is continuously recycled. To prevent the deterioration of water quality, the water is treated mechanically through the removal of particulate matter and biologically through the conversion of harmful accumulated chemicals into non-toxic ones.

Other treatments such as UV sterilization, ozonation, and oxygen injection are also utilized to maintain optimal water quality. Through this system, many of the environmental drawbacks of aquaculture are minimized including escaped fish, water usage, and the introduction of harmful pollutants. The practices also increase efficiency of feed utilisation and growth by providing optimal water quality parameters.

One of the drawbacks to recirculating aquaculture systems is water exchange. However, the rate of water exchange can be reduced through aquaponics, such as the incorporation of hydroponically grown plants and denitrification. Both methods reduce the amount of nitrate in the water, and can potentially eliminate the need for water exchanges, closing the aquaculture system from the environment. The amount of interaction between the aquaculture system and the environment can be measured through the cumulative feed burden (CFB kg/M_3), which measures the amount of feed that goes into the RAS relative to the amount of water and waste discharged.

Because of its high capital and operating costs, RAS has generally been restricted to practices such as broodstock maturation, larval rearing, fingerling production, research animal production, the SPF (specific pathogen free) animal production, and caviar and ornamental fish production. Although the use of RAS for other species is considered by many aquaculturalists to be impractical, there has been some limited successful implementation of this with high value product such as barramundi, sturgeon and live tilapia in the U.S.A.

Fish as Food

Fish as food describes the edible parts of freshwater and saltwater-dwelling, cold-blooded vertebrates with gills. Shellfish, such as mollusks and crustaceans, are other edible water-dwelling animals that fall into the broadest category of fish.

Consumption

Fish is consumed as food all over the world; with other seafoods, it provides the world's prime source of high-quality protein: 14-16% of the animal protein consumed world-wide; over one billion people rely on fish as their primary source of animal protein. Fish is among the most common food allergens.

Iceland, Japan and Portugal are the greatest consumers of fish per capita in the world.

Common Species

There are over 27,000 species of fish, making them the most diverse group of vertebrates. However, only a small number of the total species are considered food fish and are commonly eaten. Some common food fish species are listed below:

- Anchovy
- Carp
- Catfish
- Cod
- Eel
- Haddock
- Herring
- Mackerel
- Patagonian toothfish
- Salmon
- Sardine
- Scad
- Snapper
- Tilapia
- Trout
- Tuna

Perishability

Fish is a highly perishable product. The fishy smell of dead fish is due to the breakdown of amino acids into biogenic amines and ammonia.

Live food fish are sometimes transported in tanks at high expense for an international market that prefers its seafood killed immediately before it is cooked. Delivery of live fish without water is also being explored. While some seafood restaurants keep live fish in aquaria for display purposes or for cultural beliefs, the majority of live fish are kept for dining customers. The live food fish trade in Hong Kong, for example, is estimated to have driven imports of live food fish to more than 15,000 tonnes in 2000. Worldwide sales that year were estimated at US$400 million, according to the World Resources Institute.

Preservation

Fresh fish is a highly perishable food product, so it must be eaten promptly or discarded; it can be kept for only a short time. In many countries, fresh fish are filleted and displayed for sale on a bed of crushed ice or refrigerated. Fresh fish is most commonly found near bodies of water, but the advent of refrigerated train and truck transportation has made fresh fish more widely available inland.

Long term preservation of fish is accomplished in a variety of ways. The oldest and still most widely used techniques are drying and salting. Desiccation (complete drying) is commonly used to preserve fish such as cod. Partial drying and salting is popular for the preservation of fish like herring and mackerel. Fish such as salmon, tuna, and herring are cooked and canned. Most fish are filleted prior to canning, but some small fish (e.g. sardines) are only decapitated and gutted prior to canning.

Preparation

Fish can be prepared in a variety of ways. It can be uncooked (raw) (cf. sashimi). It can be cured by marinating (cf. escabeche), pickling (cf. pickled herring), or smoking (cf. smoked salmon). Or it can be cooked by baking, frying (cf. fish and chips), grilling, poaching (cf. court-bouillon), or steaming. Many of the preservation techniques used in different cultures have since become unnecessary but are still performed for their resulting taste and texture when consumed.

Nutrition and Health

Fish, especially saltwater fish, is high in Omega 3 fatty acids, which are heart-friendly, and a regular diet of fish is highly recommended by nutritionists This is supposed to be one of the major causes of reduced risk for cardiovascular diseases in Eskimos. It has been suggested that the longer lifespan of Japanese and Nordic populations may be partially due to their higher consumption of fish and seafood. The Mediterranean diet is likewise based on a rich intake of fish.

Demersal fish output in 2005 Fish products have been shown to contain varying amounts of heavy metals, particularly mercury and fat-soluble pollutants from water pollution. According to the US Food and Drug Administration (FDA), the risk from mercury by eating fish and shellfish is not a health concern for most people . However, certain seafood contains sufficient mercury to harm an unborn baby or young child's developing nervous system. The FDA makes three recommendations for child-bearing women and young children:

1. Do not eat Shark, Swordfish, King Mackerel, or Tilefish because they contain high levels of mercury.
2. Eat up to 12 ounces (2 average meals) a week of a variety of fish and shellfish that are lower in mercury. Five of the most commonly eaten fish that are low in mercury are shrimp, canned light tuna, salmon, pollock, and catfish. Another commonly eaten fish, albacore ("white") tuna has more mercury than canned light tuna. So, when choosing your two meals of fish and shellfish, you may eat up to 6 ounces (one average meal) of albacore tuna per week.
3. Check local advisories about the safety of fish caught by family and friends in your local lakes, rivers, and coastal areas. If no advice is available, eat up to 6 ounces (one average meal) per week of fish you catch from local waters, but don't consume any other fish during that week.

These recommendations are also advised when feeding fish and shellfish to young children, but in smaller portions

Parasites in fish are a natural occurrence and common. Though not a health concern in thoroughly cooked fish, parasites are a concern when consumers eat raw or lightly preserved fish such as sashimi, sushi, ceviche, and gravlax. The popularity of the such raw fish dishes makes it important for consumers to be aware of this risk. Raw fish should be frozen to an internal temperature of -20°C (-4°F) for at least 7 days to kill parasites. It is important to be aware that home freezers may not be cold enough to kill parasites.

Traditionally, fish that live some or part of their lives in fresh water were considered unsuitable for sashimi due to the possibility of parasites. Parasitic infections from freshwater fish are a serious problem in some parts of the world, particularly Southeast Asia. Fish that spend part of their life cycle in brackish or freshwater, like salmon are a particular problem. A study in Seattle, Washington showed that 100% of wild salmon had roundworm larvae capable of infecting people. In the same study farm raised salmon did not have any roundworm larvae. Fish are the most common food to obstruct the airway and cause choking which was responsible for about 4,500 accidents a year in the U.K. as of 1998.

Fish as Meat

The term "meat" has animal, vegetable and fungal applications - to wit, the "meat" of a tomato (distinct from the juice and seeds), the "meat" of a mushroom cap (as distinct from spores, gills and stems); and the edible flesh of any animal, as well as its edible organs (both as distinct from the bones, skin, feathers, fur, scales, etc.), are called "meat".

As a generic culinary and butchery term, "meat" refers to the muscular flesh of a mammal. This is the definition most commonly applied by governments in meat product regulation and food labeling, and in religious rites and rituals. Edible birds and fish/seafood are not "meat" under this application but are treated separately from mammals. Likewise, amphibians and reptiles, not to mention the "meat" of edible insects, arachnids, and so on

Religious rites and rituals regarding food also tend to apply this distinction, classifying the birds of the air and the fish of the sea separately from land-bound mammals. Sea-bound mammals are often treated as fish under religious laws - as in Jewish dietary law, which forbids the eating of whale, dolphin, porpoise, and orca because they are not "fish with fins and scales"; nor, as mammals, do they "cheweth the cud and divideth the hoof."

Otherwise, seasonal religious prohibitions against eating meat do not usually include fish. For example, meat was forbidden during Lent and on all Fridays of the year in pre-Vatican II Roman Catholicism, but fish was permitted (as were eggs). In Eastern Orthodoxy, fish is permitted on some fast days when meat is forbidden, but stricter fast days also prohibit fish with fins and scales, while permitting invertebrate seafood such as shrimp and oysters, considering them "fish without blood.

Muslim (*halaal*) and Jewish (*kosher*) practise treat fish differently from other animal foods. Some Buddhists and Hindus (Brahmins of West Bengal in India) abjure meat, but not fish. From a Buddhist point of view, if a person abjures meat, he or she is most likely to abjure fish as well. Fish is also meat since it comes from animal.

Pescetarians, for example, may consume fish based solely upon the fact that the fish are not factory farmed as land animals are (i.e., their problem is with the capitalist-industrial production of meat, not with the consumption of animal foods themselves). Some eat fish with the justification that fish have less sophisticated nervous systems than land-dwelling animals. Others may choose to consume only wild fish based upon the lack of confinement, while choosing to not consume fish that have been farmed.

Mercury Content

Fish and shellfish have a natural tendency to concentrate mercury in their bodies, often in the form of methylmercury, a highly toxic organic compound of mercury. Species of fish that are high on the food chain, such as shark, swordfish, king mackerel, albacore tuna, and tilefish contain higher concentrations of mercury than others. This is because mercury is stored in the muscle tissues of fish, and when a predatory fish eats another fish, it assumes the entire body burden of mercury in the consumed fish. Since fish are less efficient at depurating than accumulating methylmercury, fish-tissue concentrations increase over time. Thus species that are high on the food chain amass body burdens of mercury that can be ten times higher than the species they consume. This process is called biomagnification. The first occurrence of widespread mercury poisoning in humans occurred this way in Minamata, Japan, now called Minamata disease.

The complexities associated with mercury transport and environmental fate are described by USEPA in their 1997 Mercury Study Report to Congress. Because methylmercury and high levels of elemental mercury can be particularly toxic to unborn or young children, organisations such as the U.S. EPA and FDA recommend that women who are pregnant or plan to become pregnant within the next one or two years, as well as young children avoid eating more than 6 ounces (one average meal) of fish per week.

In the United States the FDA has an action level for methyl mercury in commercial marine and freshwater fish that is 1.0 parts per million (ppm), and in Canada the limit for the total of mercury content is 0.5 ppm. The Got Mercury? website includes a calculator for determining mercury levels in fish.

Species with characteristically low levels of mercury include shrimp, tilapia, salmon, pollock, and catfish (FDA March 2004). The FDA characterizes shrimp, catfish, pollock, salmon, and canned light tuna as low-mercury seafood, although recent tests have indicated that up to 6 per cent of canned light tuna may contain high levels.

13

Marine Conservation and Biology

CONSERVATION

Introduction

Marine conservation, also known as marine resources conservation, is the protection and preservation of ecosystems in oceans and seas. Marine conservation focuses on limiting human-caused damage to marine ecosystems, and on restoring damaged marine ecosystems. Marine conservation also focuses on preserving vulnerable marine species.

Overview

Marine conservation is the study of conserving physical and biological marine resources and ecosystem functions. This is a relatively new discipline. Marine conservationists rely on a combination of scientific principles derived from marine biology, oceanography, and fisheries science, as well as on human factors such as demand for marine resources and marine law, economics and policy in order to determine how to best protect and conserve marine species and ecosystems. Marine conservation can be seen as a subdiscipline of conservation biology.

Techniques

Strategies and techniques for marine conservation tend to combine theoretical disciplines, such as population biology, with practical conservation strategies, such as setting up protected areas, as with marine protected areas (MPAs) or Voluntary Marine Conservation Areas. Other techniques include developing sustainable fisheries and restoring the populations of endangered species through artificial means.

Another focus of conservationists is on curtailing human activities that are detrimental to either marine ecosystems or species through policy, techniques such as fishing quotas, like those set up by the Northwest Atlantic Fisheries Organisation, or laws such as those listed below. Recognizing the economics involved in human use of marine ecosystems is key, as is education of the public about conservation issues.

LAWS AND TREATIES

International laws and treaties related to marine conservation include the 1966 Convention on Fishing and Conservation of Living Resources of the High Seas. United States laws related to marine conservation include the 1972 Marine Mammal Protection Act, as well as the 1972 Marine Protection, Research and Sanctuaries Act which established the National Marine Sanctuaries programme.

ORGANISATIONS AND EDUCATION

There are marine conservation organisations throughout the world that focus on funding conservation efforts, educating the public and stakeholders, and lobbying for conservation law and policy. Examples of these organisations are the Blue Frontier Campaign (United States), Frontier (the Society for Environmental Exploration) (United Kingdom), and Marine Conservation Society (United Kingdom).

On a regional level, PERSGA the Regional Organisation for the Conservation of the Environment of the Red Sea and the Gulf of Aden, is a regional entity serves as the secretariat for the Jeddah Convention-1982, one of the first regional marine agreements. PERSGA Member States are: Djibouti, Egypt, Jordan, Saudi Arabia, Somalia, Sudan and Yemen.

Marine biology is the scientific study of living organisms in the ocean or other marine or brackish bodies of water. Given that in biology many phyla, families and genera have some species that live in the sea and others that live on land, marine biology classifies species based on the environment rather than on taxonomy. Marine biology differs from marine ecology as marine ecology is focused on how organisms interact with each other and environment and biology is the study of the animal itself.

Marine life is a vast resource, providing food, medicine, and raw materials, in addition to helping to support recreation and tourism all over the world. At a fundamental level, marine life helps determine the very nature of our planet. Marine organisms contribute significantly to the oxygen cycle, and are involved in the regulation of the earth's climate. Shorelines are in part shaped and protected by marine life, and some marine organisms even help create new land.

Marine biology covers a great deal, from the microscopic, including most zooplankton and phytoplankton, where zooplankton can be as small as 0.02 micrometers or as big as 2 metres in the case of the sunfish to the huge cetaceans (whales) which reach up to a reported 48 metres (125 feet) in length.

The habitats studied by marine biology include everything from the tiny layers of surface water in which organisms and abiotic items may be trapped in surface tension between the ocean and atmosphere, to the depths of the abyssal trenches, sometimes 10,000 metres or more beneath the surface of the ocean. It studies habitats such as coral reefs, kelp forests, tidepools, muddy, sandy and rocky bottoms, and the open ocean (pelagic) zone, where solid objects are rare and the surface of the water is the only visible boundary.

A large amount of all life on Earth exists in the oceans. Exactly how large the proportion is still unknown. While the oceans comprise about 71% of the earth's surface, due to their depth they encompass about 300 times the habitable volume of the terrestrial habitats on earth.

Many species are economically important to humans, including food fish. It is also becoming understood that the well-being of marine organisms and other organisms are linked in very fundamental ways. The human body of knowledge regarding the relationship between life in the sea and important cycles is rapidly growing, with new discoveries being made nearly every day. These cycles include those of matter (such as the carbon cycle) and of air (such as earth's respiration, and movement of energy through ecosystems including the ocean). Large areas beneath the ocean surface still remain effectively unexplored.

Subfields

The marine ecosystem is large, and thus there are many subfields of marine biology. Most involve studying specializations of particular animal groups. (i.e. phycology, invertebrate zoology and ichthyology). Other subfields study the physical effects of continual immersion in sea water and the ocean in general, adaptation to a salty environment, and the effects of changing various oceanic properties on marine life. A subfield of marine biology studies the relationships between oceans and ocean life, and global warming and environmental issues (such as carbon dioxide displacement). Recent marine biotechnology has focused largely on marine biomolecules, especially proteins, that may have uses in medicine or engineering. Marine environments are the home to many exotic biological materials that may inspire biomimetic materials.

Related Fields

Marine biology is a branch of oceanography and is closely linked to biology. It also encompasses many ideas from ecology. Fisheries science and marine conservation can be considered partial offshoots of marine biology.

Microscopic Life

Microscopic life undersea is incredibly diverse and still poorly understood. For example, the role of viruses in marine ecosystems is barely being explored even in the beginning of the 21st century.

The role of phytoplankton is better understood due to their critical position as the most numerous primary producers on earth. Phytoplankton are categorized into cyanobacteria (also called blue-green algae/bacteria), various types of algae (red, green, brown, and yellow-green), diatoms, dinoflagellates, euglenoids, coccolithophorids, cryptomonads, chrysophytes, chlorophytes, prasinophytes, and silicoflagellates.

Zooplankton tend to be somewhat larger, and not all are microscopic. Many protozoa are zooplankton, including dinoflagellates, zooflagellates, foraminiferans, and radiolarians. Some of these (such as dinoflaggelates) are also phytoplankton; the plant/animal distinction often breaks down in very small organisms. Other zooplankton include cnidarians, ctenophores, chaetognaths, molluscs, arthropods, urochordates, and annelids such as polychaetes. Many larger animals begin their life as zooplankton before they become large enough to take their familiar forms.

Plants and Algae

Plant life is relatively rare under sea. Most of the niche occupied by sub-plants on land is actually occupied by macroscopic algae in the ocean, such as Sargassum and kelp, which are commonly known as seaweeds that create kelp forests. The non algae plants that do survive in the sea are often found in shallow waters, such as the seagrasses (examples of which are eelgrass, Zostera, and turtle grass, Thalassia). These plants have adapted to the high salinity of the ocean environment. The intertidal zone is also a good place to find plant life in the sea, where mangroves or cordgrass or beach grass might grow. Sea kelp is very important to small sea creatures because the creatures can hide from predators. Eel grass is the most important. It is where hairing and other small fish live to escape from predators.

Marine Invertebrates

As on land, invertebrates make up a huge portion of all life in the sea. Invertebrate sea life includes Cnidaria such as jellyfish and sea anemones; Ctenophora; sea worms including the phyla Platyhelminthes, Nemertea, Annelida, Sipuncula, Echiura, Chaetognatha, and the Phoronida; Mollusca including shellfish, squid, octopus; Crustacea; Porifera; Bryozoa; Echinodermata including starfish; and Urochordete - sea squirts or tunicates.

Fish

Fish have evolved very different biological functions from other large organisms. Fish anatomy includes a two-chambered heart, operculum, secretory cells that produce mucous, swim bladder, scales, fins, lips and eyes. Fish breathe by extracting oxygen from water through their gills. Fins propel and stabilize the fish in the water. Well known fish include: sardines, anchovy, ling cod, clownfish (also known as anemonefish), and bottom fish which include halibut or ling cod. Predators include sharks and barracuda.

Reptiles

Reptiles which inhabit or frequent the sea include sea turtles, Marine Iguana, sea snakes, and Saltwater Crocodiles. Most extant marine reptiles, except for some sea snakes are oviparous and need to return to land to lay their eggs. Thus most species, excepting sea turtles, live on or near land rather than in the ocean. Some extinct marine reptiles, such as ichthyosaurs, evolved to be viviparous and had no requirement to return to land.

Seabirds

Seabirds are species of birds adapted to living in the marine environment, examples including albatross, penguins, gannets, and auks. Although they spend most of their lives in the ocean, species such as gulls can often be found thousands of miles inland.

Marine Mammals

There are five main types of marine mammals:

- Cetaceans include toothed whales (Suborder Odontoceti), such as the Sperm Whale, dolphins, and porpoises such as the Dall's porpoise. Cetaceans also include baleen whales (*Suborder mysticeti*), such as the Gray Whale, Humpback Whale, and Blue Whale.

- Sirenians include manatees, the Dugong, and the extinct Steller's Sea Cow.
- Seals (Family *Phocidae*), sea lions (Family *Otariidae* - which also include the fur seals), and the Walrus (Family *Odobenidae*) are all considered pinnipeds.
- The Sea Otter is a member of the Family *Mustelidae*, which includes weasels and badgers.
- The Polar Bear (Family *Ursidae*) is sometimes considered a marine mammal because of its dependence on the sea.

Reefs

Reefs comprise some of the densest and most diverse habitats in the world. The best-known types of reefs are tropical coral reefs which exist in most tropical waters; however, reefs can also exist in cold water. Reefs are built up by corals and other calcium-depositing animals, usually on top of a rocky outcrop on the ocean floor. Reefs can also grow on other surfaces, which has made it possible to create artificial reefs. Coral reefs also support a huge community of life, including the corals themselves, their symbiotic zooxanthellae, tropical fish and many other organisms.

Much attention in marine biology is focused on coral reefs and the El Niño weather phenomenon. In 1998, coral reefs experienced a "once in a thousand years" bleaching event, in which vast expanses of reefs across the Earth died because sea surface temperatures rose well above normal. Some reefs are recovering, but scientists say that 58% of the world's coral reefs are now endangered and predict that global warming could exacerbate this trend.

Deep Sea and Trenches

The deepest recorded oceanic trenches measure to date is the Mariana Trench, near the Philippines, in the Pacific Ocean at 10924 m (35838 ft). At such depths, water pressure is extreme and there is no sunlight, but some life still exists.

Small flounder (family Soleidae) fish and shrimp were seen by the American crew of the bathyscaphe Trieste when it dove to the bottom in 1960. Other notable oceanic trenches include Monterey Canyon, in the eastern Pacific, the Tonga Trench in the southwest at 10,882 m (35,702 ft), the Philippine Trench, the Puerto Rico Trench at 8605 m (28232 ft), the Romanche Trench at 7760 m (24450 ft), Fram Basin in the Arctic Ocean at 4665 m (15305 ft), the Java Trench at 7450 m (24442 ft), and the South Sandwich Trench at 7235 m (23737 ft).

In general, the deep sea is considered to start at the aphotic zone, the point where sunlight loses its power of transference through the water. Many life forms that live at these depths have the ability to create their own light. Much life centers on seamounts that rise from the depths, where fish and other sea life congregate to spawn and feed. Hydrothermal vents along the mid-ocean ridge spreading centers act as oases, as do their opposites, cold seeps. Such places support unique biomes and many new microbes and other lifeforms have been discovered at these locations.

Open Ocean

The great expanse of open ocean habitat is huge, and many species can be found passing through it and living in it. The term "open ocean" usually is meant to refer to the vast stretches of water between points of land, or between undersea mounts. Contrary to popular notions the open ocean is often not the place where marine animals spend the majority of their lives. Most species simply pass through the open ocean on their ways to other places. Larger species are the main ongoing inhabitants.

Intertidal and Shore

Intertidal zones, those areas close to shore, are constantly being exposed and covered by the ocean's tides. A huge array of life lives within this zone.

Shore habitats span from the upper intertidal zones to the area where land vegetation takes prominence. It can be underwater anywhere from daily to very infrequently. Many species here are scavengers, living off of sea life that is washed up on the shore. Many land animals also make much use of the shore and intertidal habitats. A subgroup of organisms in this habitat bores and grinds exposed rock through the process of bioerosion.

Distribution Factors

An active research topic in marine biology is to discover and map the life cycles of various species and where they spend their time. Marine biologists study how the ocean currents, tides and many other oceanic factors affect ocean lifeforms, including their growth, distribution and well-being. This has only recently become technically feasible with advances in GPS and newer underwater visual devices. Most ocean life breeds in specific places, nests or not in others, spends time as juveniles in still others, and in maturity in yet others. Scientists know little about where many species spend different parts of their life cycles. For example, it is still largely unknown where sea turtles and some sharks travel. Tracking devices do not work for some life forms, and the ocean is not friendly to technology. This is important to scientists and fishermen because they are discovering that by restricting commercial fishing in one small area they can have a large impact in maintaining a healthy fish population in a much larger area far away.

WATER POLLUTION

Water pollution is the contamination of water bodies such as lakes, rivers, oceans, and groundwater caused by human activities, which can be harmful to organisms and plants that live in these water bodies.

Water pollution is a major problem in the global context. It has been suggested that it is the leading worldwide cause of deaths and diseases, and that it accounts for the deaths of more than 14,000 people daily. In addition to the acute problems of water pollution in developing countries, industrialized countries continue to struggle with pollution problems as well. In the most recent national report on water quality in the

United States, 45 percent of assessed stream miles, 47 percent of assessed lake acres, and 32 percent of assessed bay and estuarine square miles were classified as polluted.

Water is typically referred to as polluted when it is impaired by anthropogenic contaminants and either does not support a human use, like serving as drinking water, or undergoes a marked shift in its ability to support its constituent biotic communities, such as fish. Natural phenomena such as volcanoes, algae blooms, storms, and earthquakes also cause major changes in water quality and the ecological status of water. Water pollution has many causes and characteristics.

Water Pollution Categories

Surface water and groundwater have often been studied and managed as separate resources, although they are interrelated. Sources of surface water pollution are generally grouped into two categories based on their origin.

Point Source Pollution

Point source pollution refers to contaminants that enter a waterway through a discrete conveyance, such as a pipe or ditch. Examples of sources in this category include discharges from a sewage treatment plant, a factory, or a city storm drain. The U.S. Clean Water Act (CWA) defines point source for regulatory enforcement purposes

Non-point Source Pollution

Non-point source (NPS) pollution refers to diffuse contamination that does not originate from a single discrete source. NPS pollution is often a cumulative effect of small amounts of contaminants gathered from a large area. Nutrient runoff in stormwater from "sheet flow" over an agricultural field or a forest are sometimes cited as examples of NPS pollution.

Contaminated stormwater washed off of parking lots, roads and highways is sometimes included under the category of NPS pollution. However, this runoff is typically channeled into storm drain systems and discharged through pipes to local surface waters, and is a point source. The CWA definition of point source was amended in 1987 to include municipal storm sewer systems, as well as industrial stormwater, such as from construction sites.

Materials and Phenomena Contributing to Water Pollution

The specific contaminants leading to pollution in water include a wide spectrum of chemicals, pathogens, and physical or sensory changes such as elevated temperature and discolouration. While many of the chemicals and substances that are regulated may be naturally occurring (calcium, sodium, iron, manganese, etc.) the concentration is often the key in determining what is a natural component of water, and what is a contaminant.

Oxygen-depleting substances may be natural materials, such as plant matter (e.g. leaves and grass) as well as man-made chemicals. Other natural and anthropogenic substances may cause turbidity (cloudiness) which blocks light and disrupts plant growth, and clogs the gills of some fish species. Many of the chemical substances are toxic. Pathogens can produce waterborne diseases in either human or animal hosts. Alteration of water's physical chemistry include acidity (change in pH), electrical conductivity, temperature, and eutrophication. Eutrophication is the fertilization of surface water by nutrients that were previously scarce.

Pathogens

Coliform bacteria are a commonly-used bacterial indicator of water pollution, although not an actual cause of disease. Other microorganisms sometimes found in surface waters which have caused human health problems include:

- Cryptosporidium parvum.
- Giardia lamblia.
- Salmonella.

High levels of pathogens may result from inadequately treated sewage discharges or livestock operations.

Chemical and Other Contaminants

Contaminants may include organic and inorganic substances.

Organic water pollutants include:

- Detergents
- Disinfection by-products found in chemically disinfected drinking water, such as chloroform
- Food processing waste, which can include oxygen-demanding substances, fats and grease.
- Insecticides and herbicides, a huge range of organohalides and other chemical compounds.
- Petroleum hydrocarbons, including fuels (gasoline, diesel fuel, jet fuels, and fuel oil) and lubricants (motor oil), from stormwater runoff.
- Tree and brush debris from logging operations.
- Volatile organic compounds (VOCs), such as industrial solvents, from improper storage. Chlorinated solvents, which are dense non-aqueous phase liquids (DNAPLs), may fall to the bottom of reservoirs, since they don't mix well with water and are denser.
- Various chemical compounds found in personal hygiene and cosmetic products.

Inorganic water pollutants include:

- Acidity caused by industrial discharges (especially sulfur dioxide from power plants).
- Ammonia from food processing waste.
- Chemical waste as industrial by-products.
- Fertilizers containing nutrients—nitrates and phosphates—which are found in stormwater runoff from agriculture, as well as commercial and residential use.
- Heavy metals from motor vehicles (via urban stormwater runoff) and acid mine drainage.
- Silt (sediment) in runoff from construction sites, logging, slash and burn practices or land clearing sites.

Macroscopic pollution—large visible items polluting the water—may be termed "floatables" in an urban stormwater context, or marine debris when found on the open seas, and can include such items as:

- Trash (e.g. paper, plastic, or food waste) discarded by people on the ground, and that are washed by rainfall into storm drains and eventually discharged into surface waters.
- Nurdles, small ubiquitous waterborne plastic pellets.
- Shipwrecks, large derelict ships.

Transport and chemical reactions of water pollutants.

Groundwater Pollution

Interactions between groundwater and surface water are complex. Consequently, groundwater pollution, sometimes referred to as groundwater contamination, is not as easily classified as surface water pollution. By its very nature, groundwater aquifers are susceptible to contamination from sources that may not directly affect surface water bodies, and the distinction of point vs. nonpoint source may be irrelevant. A spill of a chemical contaminant on soil, located away from a surface water body, may not necessarily create point source or non-point source pollution, but nonetheless may contaminate the aquifer below. Analysis of groundwater contamination may focus on soil characteristics and hydrology, as well as the nature of the contaminant itself.

Environment Portal

Most water pollutants are eventually carried by rivers into the oceans. In some areas of the world the influence can be traced hundred miles from the mouth by studies using hydrology transport models. Advanced computer models such as SWMM or the DSSAM Model have been used in many locations worldwide to examine the fate of pollutants in aquatic systems. Indicator filter feeding species such as copepods have also been used to study pollutant fates in the New York Bight, for example. The highest toxin loads are not directly at the mouth of the Hudson River, but 100 kilometres south, since several days are required for incorporation into planktonic tissue. The Hudson discharge flows south along the coast due to coriolis force. Further south then are areas of oxygen depletion, caused by chemicals using up oxygen and by algae blooms, caused by excess nutrients from algal cell death and decomposition. Fish and shellfish kills have been reported, because toxins climb the food chain after small fish consume copepods, then large fish eat smaller fish, etc. Each successive step up the food chain causes a stepwise concentration of pollutants such as heavy metals (e.g. mercury) and persistent organic pollutants such as DDT. This is known as biomagnification, which is occasionally used interchangeably with bioaccumulation.

The North Pacific Gyre for example has collected the so-called "Great Pacific Garbage Patch" that is now estimated at 100 times the size of Texas. Many of these long-lasting pieces wind up in the stomachs of marine birds and animals. This results in obstruction of digestive pathways which leads to reduced appetite or even starvation.

Many chemicals undergo reactive decay or chemically change especially over long periods of time in groundwater reservoirs. A noteworthy class of such chemicals is the chlorinated hydrocarbons such as trichloroethylene (used in industrial metal degreasing and electronics manufacturing) and tetrachloroethylene used in the dry cleaning industry (note latest advances in liquid carbon dioxide in dry cleaning that avoids all use of chemicals). Both of these chemicals, which are carcinogens themselves, undergo partial decomposition reactions, leading to new hazardous chemicals (including dichloroethylene and vinyl chloride).

Groundwater pollution is much more difficult to abate than surface pollution because groundwater can move great distances through unseen aquifers. Non-porous aquifers such as clays partially purify water of bacteria by simple filtration (adsorption and absorption), dilution, and, in some cases, chemical reactions and biological activity: however, in some cases, the pollutants merely transform to soil contaminants. Groundwater that moves through cracks and caverns is not filtered and can be transported as easily as surface water. In fact, this can be aggravated by the human tendency to use natural sinkholes as dumps in areas of Karst topography.

There are a variety of secondary effects stemming not from the original pollutant, but a derivative condition. Some of these secondary impacts are:

- Silt-bearing surface runoff from can inhibit the penetration of sunlight through the water column, hampering photosynthesis in aquatic plants.
- Thermal pollution can induce fish kills and invasion by new thermophilic species. This can cause further problems to existing wildlife.

Measurement of Water Pollution

Water pollution may be analyzed through several broad categories of methods: physical, chemical and biological. Most methods involve collection of samples, followed by specialized analytical tests. Some methods may be conducted *in situ*, without sampling, such as temperature. Government agencies and research organisations have published standardized, validated analytical test methods to facilitate the comparability of results from disparate testing events.

Sampling

Sampling of water for physical or chemical testing can be done by several methods, depending on the accuracy needed and the characteristics of the contaminant. Many contamination events are sharply restricted in time, most commonly in association with rain events. For this reason "grab" samples are often inadequate for fully quantifying contaminant levels. Scientists gathering this type of data often employ auto-sampler devices that pump increments of water at either time or discharge intervals. Sampling for biological testing involves collection of plants and/or animals from the surface water body. Depending on the type of assessment, the organisms may be identified for biosurveys (population counts) and returned to the water body, or they may be dissected for bioassays to determine toxicity.

Physical Testing

Common physical tests of water include temperature, solids concentration (e.g. total suspended solids), and turbidity.

Chemical Testing

Water samples may be examined using the principles of analytical chemistry. Many published test methods are available for both organic and inorganic compounds. Frequently-used methods include pH, biochemical oxygen demand (BOD), chemical oxygen demand (COD), nutrients (nitrate and phosphorus compounds), metals (including copper, zinc, cadmium, lead and mercury), oil and grease, total petroleum hydrocarbons (TPH), and pesticides.

Regulatory Framework

In developed countries, the primary focus of legislation and efforts to curb water pollution for the past several decades was first aimed at point sources. As many point sources have been effectively regulated—principally factories and sewage treatment plants—greater attention has been placed on controlling municipal and industrial stormwater discharges, and NPS contributions.

United Kingdom

In the UK there are common law rights (civil rights) to protect the passage of water across land unfettered in either quality of quantity. Criminal laws dating back to the 16th century exercised some control over water pollution but it was not until the River (Prevention of pollution) Acts 1951-1961 were enacted that any systematic control over water pollution was established. These laws were strengthened and extended in the Control of Pollution Act 1984 which has since been updated and modified by a series of further acts. It is a criminal offense to either pollute a lake, river, groundwater or the sea or to discharge any liquid into such water bodies without proper authority. In England and Wales such permission can only be issued by the Environment Agency and in Scotland by SEPA.

United States

In the USA, concern over water pollution resulted in the enactment of state anti-pollution laws in the latter half of the 19th century, and federal legislation enacted in 1899. The Refuse Act of the federal Rivers and Harbors Act of 1899 prohibits the disposal of any refuse matter from into either the nation's navigable rivers, lakes, streams, and other navigable bodies of water, or any tributary to such waters, unless one has first obtained a permit. The Water Pollution Control Act, passed in 1948, gave authority to the Surgeon General to reduce water pollution. However, this law did not lead to major reductions in pollution.

Growing public awareness and concern for controlling water pollution led Congress to carry out a major re-write of water pollution law in 1972. The Federal Water Pollution Control Act Amendments of 1972, commonly known as the Clean Water Act (CWA), established the basic mechanisms for controlling point source pollution The law mandated the United States Environmental Protection Agency (EPA) to publish and enforce wastewater standards for industry and municipal sewage treatment plants. The Act also continued requirements that EPA and states issue water quality standards for surface water bodies. Congress included authorization in the Act for major public financing to build municipal sewage treatment plants. The 1972 CWA, however, did not require similar regulatory standards for non-point sources.

In 1987, Congress expanded the coverage of the CWA with enactment of the Water Quality Act These amendments defined both municipal and industrial stormwater discharges as point sources and required these facilities to obtain discharge permits. The 1987 law also re-organized the public financing of municipal treatment projects and created a non-point source demonstration grant programme. Further amplification of the CWA included the enactment of the Great Lakes Legacy Act of 2002.

14

AQUACULTURE

INTRODUCTION

Aquaculture is the farming of freshwater and saltwater organisms including molluscs, crustaceans and aquatic plants. Unlike fishing, aquaculture, also known as aquafarming, implies the cultivation of aquatic populations under controlled conditions. Mariculture refers to aquaculture practiced in marine environments. Particular kinds of aquaculture include algaculture (the production of kelp/seaweed and other algae), fish farming, shrimp farming, oyster farming, and the growing of cultured pearls. Particular methods include aquaponics, which integrates fish farming and plant farming.

History

Aquaculture has been used in China since circa 2500 BC. When the waters lowered after river floods, some fishes, mainly carp, were held in artificial lakes. Their brood were later fed using nymphs and silkworm feces, while the fish themselves were eaten as a source of protein. By a fortunate genetic mutation, this early domestication of carp led to the development of goldfish in the Tang Dynasty.

The Hawaiian people practised aquaculture by constructing fish ponds. A remarkable example from ancient Hawaii is the construction of a fish pond, dating from at least

1,000 years ago, at Alekoko. According to legend, it was constructed by the mythical Menehune. The Japanese practised cultivation of seaweed by providing bamboo poles and, later, nets and oyster shells to serve as anchoring surfaces for spores. The Romans often bred fish in ponds.

The practice of aquaculture gained prevalence in Europe during the Middle Ages, since fish were scarce and thus expensive. However, improvements in transportation during the 19th century made fish easily available and inexpensive, even in inland areas, causing a decline in the practice. When the first North American fish hatchery was constructed on Dildo Island, Newfoundland Canada in 1889, it was the largest and most advanced in the world.

Americans were rarely involved in aquaculture until the late 20th century, but California residents harvested wild kelp and made legal efforts to manage the supply starting circa 1900, later even producing it as a wartime resource

Tilapia, a commonly farmed fish due to its adaptabilityActually, there was keen interest in aquaculture in the United States as early as 1859 when Stephen Ainsworth of West Bloomfield, NY began his experiments with brook trout. By 1864 Seth Green had established a commercial fish hatching operation at Caledonia Springs, near Rochester, NY. By 1866, with the involvement of Dr. W. W. Fletcher of Concord Mass, artificial fish hatching operations were under way in both Canada and the United States.

In contrast to agriculture, the rise of aquaculture is a contemporary phenomenon. According to professor Carlos M. Duarte about 430 (97%) of the aquatic species presently in culture have been domesticated since the start of the 20th century, and an estimated 106 aquatic species have been domesticated over the past decade. The domestication of an aquatic species typically involves about a decade of scientific research. Current success in the domestication of aquatic species results from the 20th century rise of knowledge on the basic biology of aquatic species and the lessons learned from past success and failure. The stagnation in the world's fisheries and overexploitation of 20 to 30% of marine fish species have provided additional impetus to domesticate marine species, just as overexploitation of land animals provided the impetus for the early domestication of land species.

In the 1960s, the price of fish began to climb, as wild fish capture rates peaked and the human population continued to rise. Today, commercial aquaculture exists on an unprecedented, huge scale. In the 1980s, open-netcage salmon farming also expanded; this particular type of aquaculture technology remains a minor part of the production of farmed finfish worldwide, but possible negative impacts on wild stocks, which have come into question since the late 1990s, have caused it to become a major cause of controversy.

World Production

In 2004, the total world production of fisheries was 140.5 million tonnes of which aquaculture contributed 45.5 million tonnes or about 32 per cent of the total world production. The growth rate of worldwide aquaculture has been sustained and rapid, averaging about eight per cent per annum for over thirty years, while the contribution to the total from wild fisheries has been essentially flat for the last decade.

ENVIRONMENTAL IMPACTS

The concentrated nature of aquaculture often leads to higher than normal levels of fish waste in the water. Fish waste is organic and composed of nutrients necessary in all components of aquatic food webs. In some instances such as nearshore, high-intensity operations, increased waste can adversely affect the environment by decreasing dissolved oxygen levels in the water column. Onshore recirculating aquaculture systems, facilities using polyculture techniques, and properly-sited facilities (e.g. offshore or areas with strong currents) are examples of ways to reduce or eliminate the negative environmental effects of fish waste.

Aquaculture can be more environmentally damaging than exploiting wild fisheries Some heavily-farmed species of fish, such as salmon, are maintained in net-contained environments.

Unused feed and waste products can contaminate the sea floor and cultured fish can escape from these pens. Escapees can out compete wild fish for food and spread disease, as well as dilute wild genetic stocks through interbreeding. The salmon consume approximately ten times more energy in fish as they are worth at harvest, making this kind of aquaculture less energy efficient than properly managed fishing.

Despite the environmental concerns, aquaculture profitability is so high that money can and should go back into promoting sustainable practices. Furthermore, new methods minimize the risk of biological and chemical pollution through minimizing stress to fish, vaccinating fish, fallowing netpens, and applying Integrated Pest Management. Vaccines also reduce antibiotic use, which are being used more and more.

Farming carnivorous fish may actually increase the pressure on wild fish, as for farming one kilo of farmed fish up to six kilo of wild fish are used for feeding

Types of Aquaculture

Algaculture

Algaculture is a form of aquaculture involving the farming of species of algae. The majority of algae that are intentionally cultivated fall into the category of microalgae, also referred to as phytoplankton, microphytes, or planktonic algae.

Macroalgae, commonly know as seaweed, also have many commercial and industrial uses, but due to their size and the specific requirements of the environment in which they need to grow, they do not lend themselves as readily to cultivation on a large scale as microalgae and are most often harvested wild from the ocean.

Fish Farming

Fish farming is the principal form of aquaculture, while other methods may fall under mariculture. It involves raising fish commercially in tanks or enclosures, usually for food. A facility that releases juvenile fish into the wild for recreational fishing or to supplement a species' natural numbers is generally referred to as a fish hatchery. Fish species raised by fish farms include salmon, catfish, tilapia, cod, carp, trout and others.

Increasing demands on wild fisheries by commercial fishing operations have caused widespread overfishing. Fish farming offers an alternative solution to the increasing market demand for fish and fish protein.

Freshwater Farming

A freshwater prawn farm is an aquaculture business designed to raise and produce freshwater prawn or shrimp for human consumption. Freshwater prawn farming shares many characteristics with, and many of the same problems as, marine shrimp farming. Unique problems are introduced by the developmental life cycle of the main species (the giant river prawn, *Macrobrachium rosenbergii*).

The global annual production of freshwater prawns (excluding crayfish and crabs) in 2003 was about 280,000 tons, of which China produced some 180,000 tons, followed by India and Thailand with some 35,000 tons each. Additionally, China produced about 370,000 tons of Chinese river crab (Eriocheir sinensis).

Integrated Multi-trophic Aquaculture

Integrated Multi-Trophic Aquaculture (IMTA) is a practice in which the by-products (wastes) from one species are recycled to become inputs (fertilizers, food) for another. Fed aquaculture (e.g. fish, shrimp) is combined with inorganic extractive (e.g. seaweed) and organic extractive (e.g. shellfish) aquaculture to create balanced systems for environmental sustainability (biomitigation), economic stability (product diversification and risk reduction) and social acceptability (better management practices).

"Multi-Trophic" refers to the incorporation of species from different trophic or nutritional levels in the same system. This is one potential distinction from the age-old practice of aquatic polyculture, which could simply be the co-culture of different fish species from the same trophic level. In this case, these organisms may all share the same biological and chemical processes, with few synergistic benefits, which could potentially lead to significant shifts in the ecosystem. Some traditional polyculture systems may, in fact, incorporate a greater diversity of species, occupying several niches, as extensive cultures (low intensity, low management) within the same pond. The "Integrated" in IMTA refers to the more intensive cultivation of the different species in proximity of each other, connected by nutrient and energy transfer through water, but not necessarily right at the same location.

Ideally, the biological and chemical processes in an IMTA system should balance. This is achieved through the appropriate selection and proportions of different species providing different ecosystem functions. The co-cultured species should be more than just biofilters; they should also be harvestable crops of commercial value A working IMTA system should result in greater production for the overall system, based on mutual benefits to the co-cultured species and improved ecosystem health, even if the individual production of some of the species is lower compared to what could be reached in monoculture practices over a short term period.

Sometimes the more general term "Integrated Aquaculture" is used to describe the integration of monocultures through water transfer between organisms. For all intents and purposes however, the terms "IMTA" and "integrated aquaculture" differ primarily in their degree of descriptiveness. These terms are sometimes interchanged. Aquaponics, fractionated aquaculture, IAAS (integrated agriculture-aquaculture systems), IPUAS (integrated peri-urban-aquaculture systems), and IFAS (integrated fisheries-aquaculture systems) may also be considered variations of the IMTA concept.

Mariculture

Mariculture is a specialized branch of aquaculture involving the cultivation of marine organisms for food and other products in the open ocean, an enclosed section of the ocean, or in tanks, ponds or raceways which are filled with seawater. An example of the latter is the farming of marine fish, prawns, or oysters in saltwater ponds. Non-food products produced by mariculture include: fish meal, nutrient agar, jewelries (e.g. cultured pearls), and cosmetics.

Shrimp Farming

A shrimp farm is an aquaculture business for the cultivation of marine shrimp for human consumption. Commercial shrimp farming began in the 1970s, and production grew steeply, particularly to match the market demands of the U.S., Japan and Western Europe. The total global production of farmed shrimp reached more than 1.6 million tonnes in 2003, representing a value of nearly 9,000 million U.S. dollars. About 75% of farmed shrimp is produced in Asia, in particular in China and Thailand. The other 25% is produced mainly in Latin America, where Brazil is the largest producer. The largest exporting nation is Thailand.

Shrimp farming has changed from traditional, small-scale businesses in Southeast Asia into a global industry. Technological advances have led to growing shrimp at ever higher densities, and broodstock is shipped worldwide. Virtually all farmed shrimp are penaeids (i.e., shrimp of the family Penaeidae), and just two species of shrimp—the Penaeus vannamei (Pacific white shrimp) and the *Penaeus monodon* (giant tiger prawn)—account for roughly 80 per cent of all farmed shrimp. These industrial monocultures are very susceptible to diseases, which have caused several regional wipe-outs of farm shrimp populations. Increasing ecological problems, repeated disease outbreaks, and pressure and criticism from both NGOs and consumer countries led to changes in the industry in the late 1990s and generally stronger regulation by governments. In 1999, a programme aimed at developing and promoting more sustainable farming practices was initiated, including governmental bodies, industry representatives, and environmental organisations.

Types of Fish in Aquaculture

- Asian carp
- Atlantic salmon
- Barramundi
- Bighead carp
- Black carp
- Catfish
- Catla
- Common carp
- Grass carp
- Gourami
- Milkfish
- Black Crappie
- Perch
- Bluegill
- Tilapia
- Mirgala, Rohita, *Lates calcrifer*

Index

G

H

I

O

P

R

S

❑❑❑